The World of Night

The World of Night

by LORUS J. MILNE

and MARGERY J. MILNE

Illustrations by T. M. Shortt

HARPER COLOPHON BOOKS

HARPER & ROW, PUBLISHERS

NEW YORK, CAMBRIDGE, HAGERSTOWN, PHILADELPHIA, SAN FRANCISCO

LONDON, MEXICO CITY, SÃO PAULO, SYDNEY

A hardcover edition of this book was originally published by Harper & Row, Publishers.

THE WORLD OF NIGHT. Copyright 1948, 1953, 1956, by Lorus J. Milne and Margery J. Milne. All rights reserved. Printed in the United States of America. No part of this book may be used or reproduced in any manner whatsoever without written permission except in the case of brief quotations embodied in critical articles and reviews. For information address Harper & Row, Publishers, Inc., 10 East 53rd Street, New York, N.Y. 10022. Published simultaneously in Canada by Fitzhenry & Whiteside Limited, Toronto.

First HARPER COLOPHON edition published 1981.

ISBN: 0-06-090839-4

81 82 83 84 85 10 9 8 7 6 5 4 3 2 1

To Esther Heacock
    and the community of friends we share

CONTENTS

APPRECIATION

THIS book has arisen, as all books should, out of a chain of happy experiences. Many of them came in the field, while we walked or sat with a flashlight in one hand.

The transitions at dusk we had described previously in an article in *Natural History* (November, 1948) as "The Twilight Shift." A sequel, "Exploring the Night," followed in the same magazine (October, 1953). We are grateful to editor Edward M. Weyer, Jr., for his friendly encouragement on this topic, and for his permission to quote freely in the present book paragraphs which were published on his pages.

Through a generous grant, the Eugene F. Saxton Memorial Trust showed confidence in our subject as suitable book material. This reassurance lifted our enthusiasm for it still farther, and we are most thankful.

At Harper & Brothers, the editor of Nature and Outdoor Books took us under his wing. To Richard B. McAdoo, his associate Hermine I. Popper, and others, go our sincerest thanks for numberless suggestions.

We would be unkind if we did not acknowledge here a great debt to our many acquaintances among the animals of the night. We apologize to those nocturnal friends for whom the chapters give no credit. In these pages we express our appreciation of their lives, and attempt to share with readers the sympathetic understanding each creature has permitted.

L.J.M. and M.J.M.

Durham, New Hampshire

The World of Night

ONE

The World of Night

MAN is a prisoner of daylight. Since prehistoric times he has striven to burst the bars by building campfires, carrying torches, inventing candles and other sources of artificial light. All of these are frail substitutes for the sun, and beyond their glow his nighttime footsteps falter. In compensation he may extend his day mentally by recounting legends, telling stories, pushing back the night by remembered or imagined excitement.

In the century before Christ, the Roman philosopher Lucretius thought back to times when even storytelling may not have begun. In his view, "like bristly boars these woodland men would lay their limbs naked on the ground, when overtaken by night time. . . . Nor did they look for daylight and the sun with loud wailing, wandering fearful through the fields in the darkness of night, until the sun with rosy torch should bring the light into the sky."

Yet many nighttime events have shaped men's lives. Even our Christian calendar dates from the first wail of a newborn child, drifting into the night where wise men watched the stars. The journey to Bethlehem of the "three kings" has led to the celebration on January 6 of Epiphany, the twelfth day —before which comes the Twelfth Night that Shakespeare immortalized. In Spain this holiday takes the place of Christmas itself.

Easter too bears the stamp of night. Each year it falls on a different date because of an ecclesiastic formula adopted in A.D. 325, as part of the Nicene Creed. In those times pilgrims trudged many miles to annual festivities in honor of the Resurrection. In Asia Minor, late March and early April were already so hot by day that the marchers preferred to travel by night. From their need for a "high held and kindly lantern" came the arithmetical computation still in vogue—the Golden Number for each year and the artificial Paschal Full Moon which determines the date of Easter.

For a city dweller, night is the time for flipping a few switches, thereby converting energy into light from electric lamps trapped as sunshine eons ago by green plants. Outside the buildings, the dust and smoke which blued the view by day, reflect a radiance from uncurtained windows, signboards, and floodlights. The moon at its fullest phase competes poorly with this city glow. Stars are scarcely seen and the Milky Way vanishes.

Even the sleepy passengers on a darkened airliner look chiefly downward at the land sweeping by below. A glare on the horizon marks a city. A few bright dots from street lamps and frame houses is a village. Beams in white and specks of red trace out the highways. Here and there these bits of web knot into traffic rotaries swirling like pinwheels. If the plane is low, the scene is the same as a flock of migrant geese would see. Yet after midnight, when the earth lights vanish one by one, only the winking red warnings on radio towers and factory chimneys, the revolving airport beacons, and the lonely headlights of some late-driving motorist show man's mark upon the land. The geese talk to one another over the city, but taxis and sanitation trucks drown out the sound.

Sometimes it is hard for us to realize the proportion of the animal kingdom that awakens at the cocktail hour, emerges into the dusk, and becomes most active in full darkness. Those animals that produce characteristic sounds or, like fireflies, bear bright beacons on their bodies, can be followed through the night hours with ease. Anyone wishing to observe nature between sunset and dawn can do so without moving from a rocking chair on a well-screened porch. He can keep his notes while stretched at length in the shelter of a tent. Or he can dose himself with mosquito repellents, fortify his eyes with a flashlight, and seek a quiet vantage point in the blackness. Each method has its advantages. Each uncovers a local and seasonal pattern of life activity— a sequence in which the birds and bugs, the beasts and crabs, meet their particular portions of the shadowed day.

In darkness the world is new and relatively unexplored. Familiar landmarks are reduced to simplicity when they are

silhouetted against a star-filled sky. Even these may disappear when a low cloud sits like a cushion upon the earth.

Winter nights can aid the human eye in watching animal activities. When snow crystals reflect a moon nearly full, the land between the horizons is like a crumpled disk of white paper with man in the middle. The frozen water crystals glitter, some of them almost as bright as the stars. This brilliance at our feet comes mainly from the moon—reaches us, in fact, from our own sun, now hidden from sight by the bulk of the earth. It is sunlight twice mirrored, once by the moon, and again by the cold blanket which mounds over low plants and lies in drifts among the trees.

In a midsummer night, the creatures active are usually far different from those of a winter evening. Yet even the date of the old English holiday called "Midsummer" varied. At first it came on July 7. "New Style" Midsummer was June 24. The halfway point between the beginning and end of the season actually falls on August 7. In any case, Midsummer became a night to dream about, when the elves and fairies were supposed to enjoy special freedom until cockcrow.

Another night has a wide appeal for children everywhere. Imagination fills the skies with broomstick-riding witches, sheeted ghosts, owls, and giant cats. At the end of harvest time and preceding November 1, All Saints' Day, or Allhallows is dedicated to any beneficent saint who might have been overlooked in the normal run of sacred days. The night before is All-Hallowe'en—the final opportunity for unplacated spirits to run about on errands of mischief.

Christmas and Twelfth Night, Midsummer and Halloween. These are the nocturnal holidays fixed in the Christian calendar. Yet few of us look out into the night itself, to wonder and observe. The people of the shadows are lesser animals, but every one is man's neighbor. Their unfamiliarity should pose no problem. But for some persons, the unknowns of night grip the mind in nameless fears. How different is this view from that of Archibald Rutledge: "One star will rob me of doubt; the dusk wind in the pines will steal away my fear; a tall oak, shivering sweetly in some little breeze and shedding odorous dew, can take away anxiety."

The vast majority of animals have waited until this time to venture forth. To man they are far less dangerous than the motor cars he dodges at noon in crossing a city's busy street. Often the most interesting facts seem just about to come to hand when the light fails. Our eyes and ears permit us to follow events in ordinary nightly darkness far more than most people realize. Looking and listening to the world around us, we can learn piece by piece. Gradually we gain a better understanding of the many living things with which we share the earth.

TWO

Nocturnal Census

In his emphasis on daylight, man allies himself with the birds and bees, the butterflies and lizards, the squirrels and monkeys, and the apes of tropical lands. It is curious that so many of these, like primitive man, are vegetarians depending chiefly on fruits, nectar, leaves, and seeds. By contrast, night hides the darker deeds, the work of fang and claw. Possibly this explains why, whenever his homeland rolls into nocturnal shadow, man restricts his activities much as do the green plants which depend for energy upon sunlight. Landscape loses its familiarity. Midnight, as Thoreau pointed out, is as unexplored as central Africa to most of us.

Usually the first night spent in a sleeping bag on the ground, or swaying in a jungle hammock between two trees, is a startling revelation—a demonstration of how much we miss by being so eye-minded. A census in the dark is far richer in kinds and individuals than is any counterpart by day.

W. H. Hudson tells of entertaining visitors from town with a demonstration of the number of nearby animals. After supper he would take them a little distance back of the house and allow them to stand still a few minutes "to feel the silence" of the pampas. Then he would fire a gun to frighten the rat-sized viscachas feeding in the grass. In a few seconds his guests would hear "an extraordinary hullabaloo, a wild outcry of hundreds and thousands of voices from all over the plains for miles around, voices that seemed to come from hundreds of different species of animals so varied they were, from the deepest booming sound to the high shrieks and squeals of shrill-voiced birds." Yet all of this uproar come from a single kind of creature which had waited until night to feed in peace.

For most animals, night ends sight. Yet even without a moon, the starlit sky produces enough illumination on fields and trails in the open woodland for man and many other animals to see remarkably well. The human eye, which can detect a seventh magnitude star or see a light of one candle-power a mile away through clear night air, can also find detail in the night's faint landscape. The brightness may be only a billionth as great as that on a sun-drenched coral beach. But once the pupils have opened wide and the most sensitive pigment has reached full concentration in the retina (a process requiring as much as 45 minutes), a person can see almost as well as an owl or a lynx, and better than a

rabbit or whippoorwill. Only animals with eyes disproportionately and actually large can gather in enough light for
even vague vision where only the illumination of stars and
night sky penetrates the undergrowth. Even on the darkest
nights, both beasts and birds of prey and their victims of
larger size can see well enough to avoid obstacles, to find or
escape from becoming food.

By the end of twilight, the night sky has dimmed to a low
brightness which is almost a physical constant—a minimum
value to be found anywhere on earth. Light scattered from
the stars by the gas molecules of air produces an over-all
illumination which is only a dim version of a noonday sky.
The blueness is there too, but the light intensity is so low that

the human eye can discern no hue. A color photograph, however, when exposed for time enough to compensate for the dimness, is just as blue of sky as when it is shot by day in a fraction of a second.

Only animals with sensitive eyes can use the brightness of the night sky as illumination. Among the vertebrates this means those with enough rod cells in the retina. Rod cells, however, yield no cues to color. It is the cone cells that provide the basis for color vision in those vertebrates whose nervous connections allow hue discrimination. When a full moon has brightened the night scene as much as possible, these cone cells—where present in a retina—begin to function. Bright moonlight permits human eyes to discern differences between red and yellow, green and blue, which are not mere brightness variation. Otherwise at night all of us are color-blind.

The long wavelengths of radiant energy that we see as red, affect our cone cells but not our rods. If a source of red illumination is intense enough to be visible at all, we know its color immediately. But many of the night-active vertebrates so limit their use of eyes to conditions of dim illumination, that their retinas are rich in rod cells to the practical exclusion of cones. As a result, it is possible to provide fairly bright floodlighting with deep red and allow human eyes to observe these creatures, without introducing any apparent change from completely normal night conditions.

Using a red-filtered automobile headlight lamp shining on the doorways of nesting tawny owls, H. N. Southern of

Oxford University Botanic Garden was able to watch through binoculars as the parents brought home food for their young. He discovered that these birds supplement their catch of meadowmice ("voles") with astonishing numbers of earth-worms—capturing them apparently by touch on nearby lawns. Since the bodies of earthworms are so soft, no one previously had even suspected their use in an owl's diet. But after the trophies were recognized in red light that the bird could not see, it was easy to demonstrate in owl droppings the characteristic bristles with which the night crawlers move around.

We depend so regularly upon our eyes that we tend to neglect the possibilities in our other senses. When we do call upon them to tell us of our surroundings in the dark, we must teach ourselves the languages of sounds and odors. Our ears can distinguish quickly between an oboe and a French horn in the sonic complexities of a symphony, but it is something else again to identify the stealthy footsteps of a fox in contrast to the occasional movement of a feeding rabbit. The snap of a twig, the flutter of displaced leaves, when contrasted with intermittent sounds from crickets and katydids, frogs and toads, strain human attention.

The calls of animals in the night are so much louder than in the daytime that they demand enlarged attention. Yet any change in them must be evaluated too. A sudden silence may be more informative than the sounds which came before.

Darkness is full of sounds. Dew dripping from leaf to leaf. The crash of a branch—perhaps broken by the weight of some climbing animal, perhaps giving way in increased humidity through the softening of a few remaining strands. From high overhead, a listener can follow the approach and departure of a honking wedge of geese. Many noises reach wakeful ears in desert, jungle, prairie, and woodland. Some are easy to identify. Others may long continue to defy knowledge and imagination. Evening sounds change character when blackness is all about. Who, earlier, would have noticed the snorts of pack horses browsing near the tent? Who would have wished them to be silent so that other noises could be more meaningful? Even the artificial has its place. Darkness lends mystery to the trilling of toads along a manmade stream in a city park.

The sounds of twilight seem particularly informative. At both close and break of day they follow a regular repertoire. Each change in light intensity is matched by the varying sounds of birds and insects.

In the night we hear the frogs and toads, the fretted wings of insects, the occasional calls of bird and mammal. And these creatures hear us, for if our voices are too loud, their calls are silenced. But hosts of other animals are about, for the most part undisturbed by human voices. And if they make sounds, we do not hear them. They may communicate in pitches beyond the reach of human ears, and respond only to calls we cannot make ourselves. The night must be full of high-pitched cries that our ears cannot record.

Each kind of animal is unique in its hearing spectrum and in the key at which sensitivity is highest. Foraging mice can communicate softly in a pitch where their voices are in-audible to predators. Distance swallows up even a slightly louder call. And sound need travel relatively few inches to be important and valuable to small creatures—permitting an animal family to stay together and alert to danger in the night—at pitches to which a cat or fox or owl is relatively in-sensitive. There is frequency range aplenty between the lowest note a man can hear and the practical upper limit of human hearing—six octaves above middle C. Yet still farther up the scale the rats and bats communicate. How high these calls extend is unknown.

To some extent the smaller the creature the higher is the frequency range of its calls and of its hearing. "For aught we know," wrote D'Arcy Thompson, "the hummingbird may sing the whole day through." For aught we know a wood-land or a prairie night may resound with intermittent calls spreading from the notes of larger birds and insects into octaves higher than any bat need use.

Whatever their hearing range, it is evident that night is the time for the timid. Nocturnal plant-eaters, such as deer, rabbits and mice cannot be seen so easily by enemies. Nor—equally important—do they face so many fearful unknowns that inhibit their urge to eat, to move, to mate. Without the sun, too, the earth loses by radiation much of its daytime heat. As temperatures drop, the relative humidity rises, and animals which are poorly protected from water-loss by evap-oration can wander more safely. Moreover, higher humid-ity and the lack of upward air currents allow odors to remain in place or to be drifted gently along the ground. Under these circumstances, the sense of smell is more useful. Sounds too, travel farther in the stiller, damper air, so that hearing comes into full play. As the light fades, emphasis shifts to calls, to odors, and as a last resort, to touch.

Animals of the night have special knowledge of their whereabouts based upon habitual use of kinesthetic sense. From explorations at a walking pace they learn that a tree is three jumps in one direction, the burrow four in another. Wherever they go in familiar territory they remain oriented by their own muscular movements. In emergency they race for safety in darkness. Six leaps and a twist to the left; three more and a sharp right turn. These directions are so thoroughly a part of routine training that they no longer mean avoidance of a stump or a rock.

Reliance on touch or smell does not necessarily imply that an animal is blind. Almost every spider has eyes, even though their use is restricted. Mice, too, have eyes; but when a mouse ventures forth at night to feed, vision furnishes almost no information. In consequence, its favorite foods are fruits or seeds which come in clusters, like a head of wheat. A few clusters furnish nourishment for twenty-four hours or more. Some may be carried home intact and provide snacks through the daylight period when open foraging involves danger. Otherwise daytime for a mouse is an interlude of essential inactivity.

Light enters the eyes of mice and men through the cornea, and passes onward to reach the sensitive cells of the retina.

Any energy not absorbed by the time it passes through the retina reaches a densely black pigment and is transformed from light into nonreflecting heat. This is the same principle that we employ when we coat the inside of a camera with black material and furnish the sensitive film with an anti-halation backing to absorb any energy that passes through the emulsion. For light must not reflect around inside a camera and reach the film again from the wrong direction, or the picture will be fogged.

The eyes of many animals which are active primarily at night, however, are unlike the visual organs of mouse and man in that they contain a mirror. At such low intensities of light as a spider or a deer must use at night, the illumination is barely enough to register on the most sensitive retina. None is left to reflect around inside. To operate at these low intensities, the eyes of the deer and many other animals, including some spiders, possess a mirror-like layer behind the sensitive cells. Any energy the retina fails to absorb and use on the inward trip is reflected through its cells once more. This gives them a second chance to capture energy and to detect a useful visual stimulus.

If a bright light is shone into an eye with a mirror backing, much of the glare is reflected out through the cornea again, back toward the headlight or flashlamp. The action is the same as that in bright buttons placed along highway curb-ings to reflect the headlight beams of each passing car. If the headlights are turned off, the reflection vanishes. There is no basis for the widespread belief that eyeshine is light which the animal projects from its eyes to illuminate its path in the dark.

Often an eyeshine discloses the unsuspected presence of an animal. One night we had camped at dusk in a New Mexican national forest and were preparing supper on our gasoline stove by flashlight. Suddenly we noticed a pair of closely set, bright orange eyes approaching. With the flashlight we found their owner to be a small bear. The animal must have been dazzled, yet it continued along a familiar path—passing between us and our tent. The only evidence that it knew we were there was an occasional backward glance as it disappeared toward the small stream. No further sign of the bear appeared, and we concluded that it had gone off down the narrow canyon. We slept perfectly. But on emerging from the tent in the morning, we discovered to our amazement a broad, well-worn trail in the dust. It circled the four walls of our canvas house and marked where the returning bear, its curiosity aroused, had paced time and again without so much as a footstep or a snort to awaken us.

Along a sea beach or through a woodland, we encounter many points of reflected light which can be identified even at a distance. A scintillating speck may be seen to move along the ground in little rushes, with pauses between. Investigation shows eyes reflecting the lamp's beam—eyes on the head of a spider. It is a daytime acquaintance, the wolf spider—a solitary creature with a dark stripe down its back—still roaming the night woods in search of insects. Across the continent in the deserts of Arizona and California there are other, larger spiders with reflecting eyes. Along back roads at night automobile headlights are picked up and thrown back by the tiny glittering eyes of trapdoor spiders, whose lidded burrows line the trails.

From the color, size and location of eyes in the night—in swamp, in field, or on an overhanging branch—the owner can often be recognized. The bullfrog glows an opalescent green. An alligator or caiman has an eyeshine so brilliantly ruby red as to merit the common backwoods name of "Ol' Fire Eyes." A whippoorwill on a branch gleams dully, but a raccoon's eyes are a bright yellow. A pair of vivid white or greenish eyeshines from a limb above the trail may prove to be a wildcat, an ocelot, or a lynx. These wild members of the cat family have eyeshines not far behind that of the domestic animal in brilliance. And what they may lack in intensity they more than make up in fearsomeness.

The presence of each predator implies the nearness of a host of smaller prey. Mice and other nocturnal rodents are so numerous, so prolific, that they form the main meat base for the native carnivores. Mice grow and mate and bear their young, serving as an essential economic link between the surplus foodstuffs of the plant kingdom on the one hand and the smaller assortment of birds and beasts of prey on the other. Through the magic of chlorophyll, the green plants trap the energy of daylight and use it to bind together atomic components drawn from air and soil moisture. Through the magic of mice and kindred small vegetarians which feed at night, the same energy is transformed whole-sale into chemical compounds a wildcat can use. Day to feed a plant. Night to feed a mouse. Night to feed a wildcat. But mouse and cat may be as silent as the plant. They vanish before dawn. Only the plant stays on for man to catalogue in his census of familiar neighbors.

THREE

Night's Measure

OVER four hundred years ago the Polish astronomer Copernicus published a new and daring idea: The earth revolves on its axis every day and circuits the sun once a year. Now we mull over the legend of Copernicus' great disciple, Galileo. Forced on pain of death to recant in public so heretical an idea, he is said to have risen slowly from his penitent knees and mumbled in his beard: *"Eppur si muove* —it moves anyway!"* Today every child learns how right Copernicus and Galileo were.

Once in twenty-four hours the earth rotates. Once a day. Why not once a *night*? Except in a polar summer, no day is twenty-four hours long. Measured from sunup to sundown, a day anywhere averages a dozen hours—no more, no less— over the span of a year. From sundown to sunup, night is twelve hours too.

To a Mohammedan minaret, day has come when the faithful can distinguish a gray thread from a white, night when neither thread can be seen at all. Astronomers employ a comparable criterion: Night is here when a seventh-magnitude star—the faintest that man's unaided eye can see—contrasts enough with the night sky to become visible. This corresponds to a position of the sun eighteen degrees below the horizon.

Country children come indoors at dusk. City dwellers caution theirs to return home when the street lights come on. Both are events of "civil" twilight—while the sun is no more than six degrees below the horizon, and the brightness of a clear sky is never less than twenty times that when the full moon is at the zenith. Following civil twilight (dusk) comes "nautical" twilight, when the brightest stars are visible, the general outlines of trees begin to grow vague, and the horizon vanishes altogether. Nautical twilight becomes night when the sun is twelve degrees below the horizon.

Only astronomers insist on a blacker sky. For them real night is far too brief. For most people the chief difficulty at the end of the year is that night seems too long, usurping hours that should belong to day. At this season man fends off the darkness with candlelight and cheery caroling, reaffirming his faith in the future.

The seeming vagueness of the boundary between day and night is an illusion stemming partly from our eyes, partly from our size, and partly from the scattered light reaching us and our surroundings from the sky. If our eyes were less sensitive or if the earth's atmosphere did not scatter so much light toward the ground after sunset, night would follow far more promptly the disappearance of the sun. Of the 1,440 minutes in an earthly revolution, the horizon needs only two to swallow up the sun itself. The moon can rise in the same length of time. Although these two bodies are so different in size (the sun's diameter is 400 times that of the moon), their distances from the earth are unlike to almost the same degree (the sun is 428 times as far away), so that to our eyes they appear to be the same size.

Since the sun is so far away and its bulk so enormous compared to that of our planet, only slightly more than 50 per cent of the earth's surface receives its radiance directly at any one time. Darkness of one kind or another envelopes the rest—bounded on all sides by sunrise and sunset. Opposite the sun, like a black skullcap on the back of the earth, is a circular patch of night covering 40 per cent of the planet's surface. Fringing the cap are three zones of twilight: astronomical, nautical, and, lastly, civil twilight, bordered all around by day.

Night does not end, even in the tropics, with the suddenness that has been credited to it. Only Kipling could make the dawn come "up like thunder outer China 'crost the Bay!" Nor does night descend again like a blanket thrown over the earth. There is time enough for eyes to become accustomed to the dark. Human pupils open wide in less than a quarter of an hour, and the retina approaches its maximum sensitivity in three times this long.

Yet at the equator, where the earth's circumference stretches for 25,000 miles, night must hurry. To travel around the world in twenty-four hours, the shadow of the earth must sweep westward at no less than 17 miles a minute—1,004 miles per hour. Our time zones reflect this fact: at each 1,004 miles of westward travel along the equator, the clock must be set back an hour. In latitudes closer to the poles the earth's circumference measured east-and-west grows progressively less, and the time-zone boundaries correspondingly narrow toward each other. All of them meet at the poles.

Longfellow was taking poetic license when he wrote, "The day is done, and the darkness Falls from the wings of Night." Night does not fall. It rises. Darkness appears first in the valleys, spreading from woodland floor to thickets. Day lasts longest in the open pasture and on the mountain peak. Distant hills clip off the setting sun at a pace as perceptible as the movement of a big clock's minute hand. White sunbeams, shorn of their blue by dust and moisture in their slanting path through the earth's atmosphere, spread a reddish glow on western hillsides. Finally the sky reflects only a baleful greenish light, unless the clouds are touched with a fleeting brilliance. Sunset has reached *their* altitude. No beams will strike the earth directly again until the dawn has come.

So gradual and impressive are these changes that we sometimes forget the vast north-south extent of this transition from day to night. For almost thirteen thousand miles, from the south polar regions to the north, the edge of the earth's shadow is engulfing the tag ends of day.

In September, down the slanting seaboard of the Atlantic coast, the lights come on in a continuous wave from New-foundland to Florida. The need for lamps reaches into Massachusetts and nearly simultaneously affects Boston's proud Beacon Hill and Concord's Walden Pond. The motor-ist crossing the Hudson at Albany, New York, turns on his headlights. Moments later the overlook lamps are brought to life at Niagara Falls. Within the hour the airport beacons glow and flash in Detroit and Chicago. A plane headed west would need to race twice the speed of sound to reach Cheyenne, Wyoming, before the darkness. Another hour and lighthouses along the Pacific coast have begun their nightly vigils.

A living transition toward night begins before the sun goes down. Rabbits, which space out their sleeping into some six-teen fairly regular naps, sense the change and become more active. Tree frogs begin to voice their penetrating, whistle-like calls. Cardinals may cease activity as much as ten min-utes before sunset, and crows settle for the night with the last rays of the sun. The next twenty minutes end the day for most of the seed- and insect-eating birds, although robins and mock-ing birds may continue to sing for as much as half an hour into twilight. Mosquitoes and fireflies appear in numbers about fifteen minutes after sunset—a little before the whippoorwills commence their calling and bats begin to write crazy pat-terns in the sky.

Nighthawks seldom leave their roosts until daylight has dwindled and their camouflage is no longer helpful. Then they climb into the upper air, alternately beating their long wings to gain altitude and coasting downward. Their cries

come back to earth at regular intervals that match the undulating flight—one cry, one pause in flapping wings. Many of them patrol a regular beat in the sky.

For a series of evenings we kept tally for half an hour or more, while one nighthawk made a seemingly irregular circuit just fourteen calls in length. The final cry coincided with a special landmark visible only to the bird. It may have been his mate. At the same spot each time, the bird took a dive, wings closed, plummeting hundreds of feet. Although we could no longer see it through the trees, the dull ringing rush of air told us when the bird braked its descent with spread pinions.

Gradually the sky assumes the anonymity of wet slate. Daytime animals have gone to sleep. A bumblebee clings to the stamens in a flower visited at the end of day. In the stone wall a few wasps hang inverted from the underside of the paper nest in which their young develop. Other adults have found crannies safe from wind, and lie with antennae curled, legs folded in repose. A number rest on sides or backs, dead to the world until the light and warmth of day reawaken them. Among the tree branches, birds of many sizes have wrapped their toes firmly around the wood. From a muscle in each thigh a strong tendon runs over the knee, down the shank, around the ankle and under the toes. In settling for the night, the body's weight pulls taut this tendon and insures a grip no wind will loosen. Not even death will dislodge them.

The sleepers may make no bed, but a surprising number return to the same site each night. It is a bedroom with neither walls nor couch. The bumblebee may be found in the identical hollyhock flower from its day of opening to the date it closes for the last time. A butterfly may select the same area of bark as a clinging place, and arrive there at dusk each day, after seemingly aimless flitting over the countryside. Birds commonly use the same roosting site for sleep, even though they have constructed an elaborate nest somewhere else. A nest is not a home but an egg-hatching device and nursery pen. It must be tended when in operation, but it has little attraction as a place to spend the night. Unless there are eggs to incubate or young to protect from the chilly dark, the nest-makers sleep elsewhere.

The anthropoid apes and man, in fact, are the most conscientious bed-builders known. The orangutang of Borneo chooses a tree top for the hours of darkness. At a height of as much as forty feet from the ground, this primate constructs of sticks a platform often four feet in diameter and flat on top. As night arrives the orangutang lies stretched on this lofty perch and reaches out with arms and legs. Fingers and toes clamp around branches as firmly as do a bird's toes, so that the animal is locked in bed, safe no matter how the tree shakes before morning.

Adult gorillas, by contrast, are too heavy to climb well. They spend their lives in family groups shuffling over the ground. Toward evening the big male bends branches together and intertwines them, often arranging a whole canopy of vines and moss. Crude knots are made of creepers—as many as two dozen to hold the tent in place. Yet neither orangutang nor gorilla family may use the same bed twice. Their feeding habits commonly exhaust the supply of tender shoots and buds nearby, and the following night finds the animals too far off for return.

Plants, too, respond noticeably to changes in light intensity. Leaves of *Oxalis*, the wood sorrel, and such members of the pea family as clover, droop against the petiole by night and are erect by day. There is no true correspondence to sleep and botanists conscientiously avoid this designation. Actually, the angle between each leaflet and the petiole changes gradually and almost continuously, reaching a maximum near noon and a minimum near midnight. This activity is not due to light alone. Clover plants, for example, will continue the same rhythmic movements for from three to five days in total darkness. In continuous light they remain erect. This curious clock-like regularity can be "taught" a plant by providing it with artificial days—say 6 hours night and 6 hours day, or 20 hours of each. Within a few cycles of exposure to these abnormal light conditions, some plants will follow the rhythm for a time in total darkness.

Wisteria leaflets and those of the bean are like clover and wood sorrel in that they droop at night. Rhododendron and grape leaves, on the other hand, turn upward and display their silvery undersurfaces, so that on a night trip through the garden these plants possess an unfamiliar brightness.

Dandelions and many other flowers of the daisy family spread their florets every day but close tightly as though to protect the precious pollen from the night's dampness. Lilies and tulips have a similar habit, although each day they may open wider than the one before. Poppies and pansies generally limit their spread condition to the daylight hours, often lasting through only a single day. Some water lilies spread their petals at sunset and remain open until noon. The pink-backed buds of evening primrose, by contrast, wait until evening, and then swell visibly. They burst open with

a little popping sound to display a butter-yellow interior. By daybreak they are wilting. Through the day the plant supports both the faded blossoms of the night before and the tightly closed buds of nights to come. Honeysuckle, too, opens its flowers in late afternoon or evening, and by dawn each has changed from a clear ivory to deep yellow.

These activities of flowers and leaves all seem based upon the same underlying type of movement. Somehow light controls many processes, including those which determine the sap pressure in cells where leaflets join their petioles. High pressure there—with turgid cells—means leaflets spread to catch the sun. Low pressure—almost wilting—lets them droop again. But why and how remain a mystery.

The length of night is subject to wide variations. For millions of years, migratory birds have been making use of this fact, whereas mankind has learned of it only within the last eight centuries. Until the days of the Crusades, human travel was chiefly east and west, or involved journeys in tropical and subtropical lands. Throughout these regions, the length of a night does remain much the same all year. But when crusaders from a foggy, northern England marched to free the Holy Land from Moslem rule, they discovered that the sun does not shine on all places in the same way.

Toward the end of June, an Arabian night in Bagdad lasts just under seven hours, if twilight is subtracted from the actual time the sun is below the horizon. At this time of year, London has no night at all. There, twilight, by astronomical definition, extends from sundown to sunup, since the sun is never so much as eighteen degrees below the horizon. Bagdad's latitude corresponds fairly well to that of New Orleans, London's to Edmonton, Alberta or central Labrador. Measured north and south these differences in latitude approximate 1,500 miles. Even in modern North America, where the major flow of traffic is east and west, few travelers have experienced such extremes in latitude.

Between the larger cities, wide variations in length of night are common. Boston, Massachusetts, and Charleston, South Carolina, are separated by a north-south distance of about 700 miles. On New Year's Day, Boston has 54 minutes less sunlight than does Charleston. But twilight almost equalizes things by extending about 30 minutes longer at that time of year in the northern city. At summer solstice, Boston's sunshine lasts a whole hour more than Charleston's, and twilight decreases full darkness by 70 extra minutes. Night is crowded into less than 4¼ hours.

At the latitude of Boston, street lamps are scarcely needed until nine o'clock standard time in summer, and twilight lasts until seven minutes before ten. Along the north shore of the Gulf of St. Lawrence (approaching the Labrador boundary), and throughout much of settled western Canada, twilight extends from sunset to sunrise. There is no real night over Lake Louise in late June and early July. These features impress the traveler, but they have even more pronounced effect on the kinds of creatures that live in various parts of the world. Indeed, one of the best reasons for moving to the north woods for the summer is that the days are longer there. Birds which know no union hours in feeding broods of hungry young are believed to make their spring migrations chiefly to take advantage of the more extended light in northern regions.

In polar lands, summer is the warm sunny season when animals depending upon daylight vision can be up and about. Since night is absent altogether there for much of the year, nocturnal creatures would have difficulties. There are fewer of them the farther north you go. But for every long summer day there is an equally extended winter night. An animal which neither migrates nor hibernates must have good vision for the long twilight and night that mark the year's end. Large eyes, large animal—and this factor of size has added importance in providing bulk of body to produce enough heat to match the winter losses from the warm body's surface. As a result, animals that brave the arctic winter and continue to be active are commonly of larger size, with thick fur and short tails—like muskox, reindeer, walrus, polar bear, and seal.

The heat of the sun is a sort of loan. It need not be given back; but it must be passed along. Over any average year, the energy received by day is dissipated through the night—radiated to space in a way that brings a balance in which life is possible. Without the regular revolution on its axis—bringing us alternately day and night—the earth would share some of the difficulty of our moon. An average six and three-quarter calories of radiant energy fall on each square inch of the earth's surface every minute, day in and day out. If all this energy were received by a single side, or if the rotation rate were much slower than at present, the temperature of the sunny face would rise to killing heights. On the shadowed side the continued loss of radiated heat would bring equally disastrous cold.

The seasons of the polar year follow closely upon the proportions of night and day. Whenever night's hours exceed those of day, there is opportunity for more loss of heat than gain. Gradually temperatures sink and winter soon prevails. Conversely, when day's length exceeds that of night, heat accumulates—more being absorbed each day than is radiated to space at night—and temperatures reach summer levels. Winter and summer depend on the divisions of light and dark. These, in turn, arise through the form of our planet and the obliquity of its axis with respect to the plane of the earth's orbit around the sun.

At equinox time in September and March, the tilt of the earth's rotational axis lies broadside to the sun, with neither pole pointing more than the other toward the source of radiant energy. In late December the north pole points away from the sun, the south pole toward the sun. In late June these relations are reversed. The tilt of the axis remains approximately constant at 23.5 degrees away from vertical, wherever the earth is in its orbit. But this constant tilt moving around the sun radically alters the distribution of energy on the earth at different times of year.

Girdling the earth's midriff is a belt nearly four thousand miles wide—the so-called Torrid Zone—between the Tropic of Cancer (at the latitude of Cuba) and the Tropic of Capricorn (just south of Rio de Janeiro). Here sun energy can meet a level surface on the earth at right angles and yield its maximum heating effect. The other extreme of the lighted region is in the polar zones. Here light never strikes a level place with *less* obliquity than 23.5 degrees. Depending on the time of year and day, and on the latitude, the angle between level earth and sun may be anywhere between this value and zero.

Not every place on earth is level. And as the surface is tilted away from the horizontal, the energy absorbed from the sun falls off rapidly. This may be due either to the slope characteristic of some particular piece of land, or to time of day—minutes or hours away from high noon. If the tilting involves only the unevenness of the earth's surface, the effect stems simply from spreading energy over a greater area. A hillside at noon in the tropics receives less heat per acre than does a level spot. In fact, a mild slope away from the sun, such as is met commonly on hilly roads—say 5 degrees, or

8.8 feet of grade in a hundred—lowers the energy received and hence the soil temperature as much as does 300 miles of travel toward the pole in terms of level surfaces.

Even where the world is level, the distribution of sun energy at any given time is uneven. The earth is not a double-sided flat expanse, flopped suddenly in toggle action from day to night. It is a spheroid—a slightly flattened ball—which rotates regularly on its axis. Where the tilting of the earth's surface with reference to the sun is due to the spheroidal form and inclination away from sunlight, the reduction in energy received suffers not only from the spreading of calories over more surface, but also from absorption of available energy by a greater thickness of the atmosphere. When the sun is directly overhead, the air blanket absorbs only about a quarter of the calories—passing 70-odd per cent to ground level. But with a low sun only 5 degrees above the horizon—as toward sundown or in a polar summer—the oblique rays pass through about eleven times as much air. A feeble one per cent of the solar energy reaches the soil, there to be distributed widely over the tilted surface.

These shapes and tilts, rotations and circuiting of the sun, contain the origins of night and day, of seasonal change and latitudinal variation. Together with one other major factor—water—they determine where a jungle, a desert, or a polar tundra can grow. They call the tune and set the pace for living things. Irregularities in the earth's surface provide the stage, with areas of land or water, with depths and slopes and altitudes.

Sands and rock grow cold and hot very quickly in shade and sun. Water's immense thermal inertia permits it to absorb and dole out prodigious numbers of calories without much change in temperature. Winds and ocean currents transport heat from place to place. Clouds restrict the night's radiation into space. And rain depends for its distribution upon water areas and winds which cross them, upon up-sloping mountain sides that elevate the moisture-laden breeze and bring on condensation. Elsewhere—on level and down-sloping land—no great amount of rain can fall. Deserts spread their sand and naked rock.

Approximate equality of night and day all year means warmth aplenty. Coupled with abundant rain, the weather specifies a land where jungle plants and animals compete for space. Without the rain and lushness of plant growth, bare earth grows intolerably hot by day. Only in the relative coolness of night are equatorial deserts active with animals which have emerged from daytime safety below the surface.

Where seasonal change has reached a point in which night is brief and daylight occupies most of the twenty-four hours in each earthly revolution, summer has come to a chilly land. Hastily the plants mature their buds and seeds. Animals reproduce their kind. Yet the number of types of each is far smaller than in a tropical jungle. Only the most resistant creatures can match the extreme variation in length of night. Some migrate. Some hibernate. A few brave the long winter when night dominates so completely over day.

Between the extremes of tropical uniformity and polar

reversals in weather are lands where night's measure runs a more temperate scale. The pendulum swing between sun calories gained and lost marks off a seasonal rhythm which never fails but seldom kills. Soils offer more to plants than where a high sun burns down on desert or rain-drenched jungle, or a low one lets all the water freeze for many months each year. Seldom have lush tropics been cradles to great civilizations. Never have the arctic lands. Man himself has found the midway band of the earth best suited to his needs. Here it is that "nature has fashioned the loveliest of earth's adornments—the ever-changing woodlands whose yearly cycle of death and renascence has evoked the wonder and gratitude of mankind since the first savage minstrel sang the first hymn to spring."

FOUR

Fresh-water Shores

NIGHT or day, wherever water laps against the land, a tangible boundary separates two worlds—one wet, one dry. Man can run along the water's edge like a sandpiper, or wade like a heron, or swim like a mink. But his ancestral line dissociated itself from aquatic life so long ago that only in early embryohood does he show marks of gill clefts like a fish. Long before he bursts from his private aquarium within his mother and ceases to depend on her lungs for his respiration, man is committed to breathing only air. Yet given opportunity, he will return time and again to the water's edge, to stare at the boundary and puzzle at the events hidden below, veiled from his eyes by reflections of the sky.

A gushing spring becomes a stream. A river meanders and cuts off oxbows. A pond fills with vegetation to transform into a marsh. Each has its water edge, its characteristic animals, its nocturnal visitors. Fittingly enough, Thoreau enjoyed fishing at night from his rowboat at Walden, "serenaded by owls and foxes, and hearing, from time to time, the creaking note of some unknown bird close at hand . . . surrounded sometimes by thousands of small perch and shiners, dimpling the surface with their tails in the moonlight." His pleasure was soul deep. His sense of kinship with wild creatures contrasted sharply with the thinking of his day. For Thoreau rejected the tenets of primitive religions without losing their wonder and acceptance of nature.

Not everyone has a Walden Pond at his doorstep. Yet most of us can find a stream or a marsh or a pond to watch as the sun goes down. Preferably it should border on a woodland, in which so many creatures find refuge for the day. Under the darkening sky they emerge one by one, as the water acquires a deceptive calm. A river seemingly ceases to flow. Only a leaf, a twig, a bit of foam sails by to show the deep current.

The dwindling of the light serves as a signal to insects in the murky depths. They rise to the surface and spread quick-drying wings, then take to the air as midges and mayflies, caddis and stoneflies. Suddenly the swallows multiply their efforts, darting in all directions. Their narrow pointed wings almost flick the water as they zigzag at high speed, snatching gnats at every twist. Above them the forest silhouette is bitten deeply by a blaze of light. Even large branches melt away when backed by the the red disc of the setting sun.

On most nights at sunset, a bat joins the late-feeding swallows. It too skims the river to reap the evening's crop of flies. But the flying mammal is merely on schedule, whereas the swallows, who should be winging toward their roosts, are striving desperately to prolong their day. Their small eyes are so inadequate in the dim light that now they miss the insects more often than they strike.

Despite the diligence of the racing birds and the toll of the active bat, most of the insects with trailing tails and opaque gray wings drift to shore and clutch the green safety of overhanging alder leaves. Those that escaped the swallows of yesterday, emerged uncaught by bats last night, ran the gauntlet through the sunny hours when vireos, wrens, warblers, and parent sparrows searched the shrubbery for them. The survivors have shed their skins a final time to reach full maturity. In the dusk their wings are clear, dry, and ready to beat the air in an intricate mating dance. The ballet will again expose them to decimation, but it will also ensure future generations.

As river banks and pond margins grow dim, a migration is in progress on the surface of the water. Jet-black, shining whirligigs which have spun and raced on the ripples all through the day, congregate for the night in quiet bays. Water striders, some large and many small, glide dry-shod to the shore with widespread "rowing oars" propelling them at a jerky pace. Out they climb, to crouch among damp fallen leaves and bits of wood debris until morning.

Behind these insects a big bullfrog may be lying spread-eagled near the bank, with eyes and eardrums extended into air. He too is listening, alert for any contestant to his territory, ready to snap up any smaller amphibian that ventures within reach. Only in the dusk can his throbbing throat be seen, lighting up like a firefly at each deep, resonating "R-r-rumph."

The time has come to watch for owls. While events on the river can still be followed easily by human eyes, these birds appear in their black recessed tree holes like so many framed portraits. They stand there, staring into the gathering night and expressing hunger by clicking noises from the down-curved beak. With the evening stars they come out, to perch inconspicuously on a horizontal branch. They puff out their feathers, making each bird far broader than the tree hole whence it came, and from time to time turn their intent stares in some new direction. The stage is set for action in the shadows.

For years we have remembered happily a single sunset and twilight experienced in the Pocono Mountains of Pennsylvania. We paused to rest on our way home, and chose a seat on a mossy bank with a forest at our backs, a river at our feet, and more woodland beyond it toward the setting sun. A solitary loon was silently fishing back and forth, the brilliance of its white throat set off sharply from the dead black of head and back and wings. Our coming did not alarm the bird; it merely moved toward the far shore. We watched it go. In the shadow of safety thrown across the river by the forest and the slanting sun, the loon's camouflage was almost perfect. In the dusk it became only a pale gray semicolon—the sole visible indication of the white neck marking—which

drifted upstream as often as down. Yet the bird was still busy, seizing any fish that rose to the surface within reach of its black, spear-like bill.

From far downstream a laughing call floated on the night air. For a moment it hung there, like a ghostly joke. The loon thirty yards away yelled a maniac's reply, and the river canyon echoed with the sudden outburst. There was no telling which was the echo, which the distant bird. A scurrying swish of water turned into a rapid rhythmic plap-plap-plap, as the nearby loon transformed from a surfaced submarine to an air-borne hydroplane, with downbeating wing tips striking the water surface. Finally, as a float-plane pilot would describe it, the loon was "on the step"—clear of the river, picking up speed in horizontal flight before zooming higher toward the distant invitation. A loon can take off only from the water. There alone the bird is able to achieve enough velocity and lift for the beating wings to overcome the earth's gravitation.

Above our heads an owl appeared in a willow tree. Our attention left it when a clump of long grass began to twitch beside a boulder near the river's edge. For a split second at a time, the hay-brown muzzle and one small shoe-button eye of a meadow mouse peered out. It was still too light, but the rodent's hunger pangs were too much for it. Soon the mouse popped out, to stand as if frozen, every muscle tensed, the insignificant tail pointing straight astern.

Peace enveloped the valley so completely that a faint brushing drew our gaze to where a doe deer stepped softly

from the woods, down toward the water's edge. She turned
her head and called gently—a soft, maternal low so quiet
that we could easily have missed it. With a little bleat, her
half-grown fawn skidded down the bank and quivered to a
halt, pressed against the mother. Both moved to the river together—the doe to drink, the fawn to stare toward the blackness of the other bank. As they stood on the sand bar, the
full length of their long legs was visible. The deer's heels
(hocks) are inconspicuously high, well within reach of the
twitching tail. The doe would have practically been ready
to swim before water reached the actual legs. It is the
slender, extended feet which raise a deer on tiptoe high
above the ground, and give it bounce and speed in the geta-
way.

In the dusk we could follow the interaction of animals
alike only in their timidity. The fawn changed position, and
stumbled on a loose rock. The meadow mouse leaped down
the doorway of its grass clump, into the dark security of a
tunnel leading to its den. The sudden rustle of dry vegetation alerted both doe and fawn. Up jerked the mother's head,
and her white tail flag stood out at half mast. With dripping
chin, she stared toward the rounded rock, the shy fawn pos-
ing identically beside her. But the four ears funneled forward
found no sequel to the sudden sound. The mouse's head came
out again. With whiskers aquiver, the little rodent was soak-
ing up courage from the serene night before making another
sally toward breakfast.

The doe led her baby back into the coolness of the woods,

where she could feed on green twigs and fallen acorns among the litter of the forest floor. Tomorrow squirrels would have a harder time finding good nuts to hide away toward the lean days of winter.

Soon we heard a dry rustling and scratchy noises on the bark of a tree where a twelve-pound porcupine was backing down the trunk from his tree-hole home. His day-long sleep was over. With clumsy lumbering gait he waddled to the river, first to drink, then to dig for the succulent roots of aquatic plants in a marshy bay.

As other interests lagged, our attention returned to the owl perched on the branch above us. Suddenly the bird shrank, its body newly sleek. It crouched, then hopped into the air on oversized down-cupped wings which beat as silently as two gobs of cotton batting rubbed together. Over the grass near the round boulder its flight stalled momentarily. The great wings rose vertically. The owl dropped like a lightning bolt, with open claws outstretched. A single squeak, the briefest rustling, and a fluff of air as the bird's pinions braked the fast descent. Once more the owl was on the wing, carrying the meadow mouse limp in its beak, back to the horizontal branch. For a minute or two we could hear snapping noises suggesting quiet satisfaction over the brief foray.

Along any fresh-water shore as the sky grows darker and the first stars appear, conflicts are evident in the gloom along the bank. From holes in the shore itself and from below the larger stones, insects emerge into the humid darkness. Ground beetles of many sizes search for mites and worms, or meat of any kind that they can subdue. In many ways they take the place of ants, lacing back and forth from the water margin into the forest. With luck, one of the larger beetles (an inch or more in length) may find a caterpillar or an unwary earth-worm. Immediately it dances around its victim, rushing in to bite, feinting and lunging, employing its two strong jaws like horizontal ice tongs. And everywhere it bites, the prey is soft enough to yield. In dealing with an earthworm, the insect must be fast, must so damage the worm's nervous system that it will be unable to withdraw into the safety of its burrow. Then the ground beetle can settle down to gorge. Smaller insects join the feast but the victor pays no attention.

In darkness, many interesting events may go unnoticed, even within a radius of fifty feet from a human observer. Animals which walk or swim or fly silently may never give away their positions. Nor is every nocturnal sound easily accounted for. At intervals a loud splash from the river may mark where a leaping fish fell back into the stream, perhaps pursued by an otter or mink. Or the otter itself may be responsible, yielding to the urge to toboggan down a muddy bank and skid into the water. Only a practiced ear can dis-tinguish these events from the sudden spank of a startled beaver's flat tail, as the dam builder dives below the surface. The round tail of a frightened muskrat can produce a dimin-utive version of the beaver's warning.

Through the night the otter slide retains its luster, proving that at least some of the plashy noises had this origin. An otter's fur is specially suited for use as a toboggan. Its durability is so outstanding that furriers rate it 100 per cent, as compared with muskrat's 45 and rabbit's 5. Seen from the front, an otter's pelt is smooth and glossy, well adapted to slipping silently through the water in pursuit of the animal's favorite food—fish of any kind. The diet is varied, however, with clams and snails, frogs and water snakes, even ducks and muskrats if starvation threatens. But so active is a healthy otter that to follow one in darkness requires patience and ingenuity. If the animal grows suspicious, it can hold its breath long enough to swim a quarter of a mile under water, then surface again without a sound.

Strangely enough, the webbing on all four feet of the otter does not mean that the animal is more aquatic in habit than the beaver (which has webbing only on the hind feet) or the muskrat (which has no webbing at all). Actually, the otter is equally at home on land and in water, and roams widely—as much as fifteen miles a night, with regular rounds over a territory sometimes fifty miles across. Beaver and muskrat, by contrast, rarely venture far from the water.

Of the three, the beaver is the best fitted for aquatic life. Not only does its oversize liver provide storage space for additional oxygenated blood, but nostrils and ears are equipped with valves which close automatically when the animal goes below the surface. It can hold its breath while working for fifteen minutes or more, four times as long as an otter. In addition, its lips are so loose and well controlled that it can draw them in and close them behind the big front

teeth to seal water from the mouth. Then the jaws can chisel
away at underwater vegetation. Beavers eat only plant food,
and as a steady diet, prefer the bark of softwood trees such
as birch, poplar, or cottonwood, aspen and willow. Toward
fall each anchors deeply in the bottom of the beaver pond
a supply of limbs and small logs to which it can come under
the ice to feed in winter.

Night is time for building and repairing beaver dams that
keep the pond from draining. These animals labor mightily,
sealing off any flowing water with a crude barricade of logs,
sticks, and mud. Often they dig long canals to the pond and
use them as channels for floating building materials cut at a

distance. Formerly beavers were valued chiefly for their pelts and these formed a standard medium of exchange. Now their importance is seen to be far greater in flood control, in conserving water so well that dry acres paralleling streams suddenly can support trees and other vegetation. Lawrence Palmer awarded the beaver a perfect citation for public service when he described it as "an animal of headwaters, where it builds $3,000 dams free."

A beaver dam may change the whole natural history of a valley. At the shore of a beaver pond, there congregate animals that would be found only rarely along the stream itself. Water lilies begin to grow, and soon may be opening their flowers at sunset, releasing fragrance into the night air, and closing again before noonday. Mud turtles swim to shore when their log-top sunbathing is ended for the day. Disturbed after dark, the reptile will draw back into its shell with a sudden hiss, its head and knees pulled into space made available only by emptying its lungs.

The raccoon hunts softer prey along the water's edge, its hand-like forepaws feeling for crayfish in the crevices. In the morning a pile of shell fragments along the shore measures its success. There the crustacean's body was manipulated under water as though to scrub it clean, then torn to shreds. The raccoon's scientific name, *Lotor*, refers to this habit of washing food.

Tracks in the bank of pond or marsh or stream show what a variety of animals walk along the margin at night. Many besides the deer come merely to drink. The bear, with its spreading sole and five toes on the ground, leaves prints suggesting those of a flat-footed man—except that the prints are in pairs. The larger (from the hind foot) lies just ahead of the smaller on each side.

Beaver prints are easy to identify, for the webbing on the hind feet marks the mud where the toes and sole come down just *behind* the spot where the front foot has left the ground.

Weasel feet are small and so much alike that their tracks seem merely pairs of paw marks—until a particularly clear impression shows that each print is actually double. The hind foot takes the place of the front almost like a second printing from a rubber stamp.

There may be many nocturnal visitors to the water's edge at one and the same time. By day each newcomer would be reluctant to advance to the shore if other large animals were visible there. But at night, surprisingly large populations can ignore nearby neighbors, though all are as close together as people in a half-filled movie house.

A few of these night-wandering animals carry lights with them. A firefly's beacon is of no value by day. In the dark it becomes a beckoning signal for another firefly. Most of the display occurs in regions of high humidity: a river bank, the swales around a pond or marsh, an open field through which a stream meanders. In many kinds, both sexes have light-producing organs below the abdomen. The male flies over places in which potential mates are perched on the tips of leaves and blades of grass. At intervals he shines his

light. If a female below signals with her glow, and if the
timing is right (indicating response to his flash and not just
another male), he turns in flight and approaches her. A
series of flashing interchanges brings him in for a landing
beside her.

The importance of the firefly's glow to the insect is clear
enough. But other sources of light are harder to account for.
Along the shore of a stream or pond under the pale illumination of the starlit sky, a brightly shining object on the sand
may appear. Usually it is several inches long and fish-like in
shape. It *is* a fish, whose dead body has a coating of light-
producing bacteria which draw attention to themselves *en
masse*. How or why is still undertermined. Some fungi produce a similar light and may surprise a walker in the woods.
The whole interior of a soggy hollow log may shine with
this "fox fire." The word "fox" in this connection signifies

mold or decay, and has no relation to the mammal seeking mice not far away.

That light should be emitted without a definite use seems strange to eye-minded man. That touch alone should be an adequate guide for an animal's course is scarcely more believable. Yet the spiral perfection of an orb-weaving spider's web and the lacework of the doily spider are engineered in the dark, strung between reeds or spread horizontally on the grassy bank, entirely by touch. In each instance the spinner pays out silk from the tip of her abdomen while, with her eight slender legs, she steps off the correct spacing from the previous thread.

Where the reeds and cattails are spaced out by shallow open water, ducks tip and dive all night to reach the vegetation along the bottom. Long-legged herons and other wading birds stand like sentinels, ready to spear a passing fish. Each finds a reason to be awake. All of them avoid the muskrats feeding among the rushes, and scatter at any sign that might indicate the approach of a hungry mink or otter. Occasionally a pale gray crow-sized bird flits overhead, its long legs dangling loosely. In full darkness its passage may be soundless. At twilight, either evening or morning, its frequent call of "Quawk" helps identify the black-crowned night heron, and gives the bird its local name.

It would be easy to conclude that these marsh birds never sleep. Yet they must, for lack of sleep kills faster than want of food. Man is not alone in his need regularly to "knit up the ravell'd sleave of care." For these creatures, in view of

their various enemies, day is the safer time to risk uncon-
sciousness, even for naps of short duration.

In its final quarter, the moon stays below the horizon
until after midnight. At its rise the quiet darkness is transformed into something new. Seen from the bank, the old
moon's light is double—one direct, the other shining from the
water's surface. Leaning trees, which Mary Webb described
as "fingering" their reflections by day, lack these companions
at night. Instead, each bare branch gives the illusion of an
unmoving comb for the rippling moonlight mirrored by the
stream.

With a bright moon some of the daytime birds awake. At
intervals they may grace the night with a clear call. The
song sparrow, the marsh wren, the redwing, even various
thrushes add their notes. The response of these birds to the
moon so resembles that of man that he often sees in the
warm-blooded, two-legged lesser creatures a kinship which
is more apparent than real. When the chilly nights of fall
approach, the birds show their uniqueness by flying south.
Man is left to record the date when the water surface
freezes.

In a winter night the frogs crouch motionless, hidden in
muddy cells well down in the bottom of the pond. Turtles
may hibernate submerged. Of the mink and otter only a
slide in the snowy bank may indicate nocturnal frolics.

Muskrats seem to have inherited the marsh. Reeds and
cattails collapse, exposing their houses to view from the
shore. Each muskrat hides within the interlacing thatch of

51

nonwoody plant material an upper chamber lined with soft grasses. From this dry haven a passage descends to the never-frozen depths of the waterway. Down the tunnel the muskrat can go in search of winter food—the bark and pith of water-lily logs and other aquatic plants—then return to shake and sleep where air can reach through the slightly porous roof.

Usually muskrats have secondary refuges burrowed deep and upward into the pond's bank. If some predator crosses the ice and tears apart the flimsy house, the muskrat can swim safely below the ice and enter an earthen sanctuary. The frost which built a bridge across the marsh hardens the soil of the bank into icy impregnability. The fox or bear usually gets nothing in return for a bout of house-wrecking. During the next thaw, when once more the marsh is open and secure, the muskrat may even return to the invaded shack and rebuild its roof and upper room.

Lengthening nights of autumn send the birds and bats to their winter homes. With shorter nights they return northward. Yet long before they reappear, man's hope leads him to search for signs of spring. He may go by moonlight, but his route should lead him to the site of last year's fresh water. It is there that the dryness of winter snow and ice melts most effectively into the stuff of summer. There, in the frosty soil along the bank, skunk cabbage shows the change of season long before the equinox. Spears of fresh green rise gradually, followed by the first flowers of the year. Willows respond with buds which swell and burst in slow motion—

as pussy and catkin, blossoms of a more delicate and fragrant sort.

None of these reassuring signals is so sudden, so unrehearsed, so enthusiastic that it can be sensed from half a mile away. Instead each must be sought out. Only the inch-long peepers, from bright throat bubbles, sing their shrill night calls for spring to come. At the boundary of wet and dry, perched on dead reeds or in icy water that would chill the ardor of almost any living thing, these amphibian mites sound their chorus. In temperate zones theirs is a resurrection long before Easter. It is a miracle dating back into the past far beyond even the softwoods and hardwoods whose buds are still clenched upon next year's leaves. Birds and bats and appreciative man were still far in the future when the first peepers proclaimed their faith in warm days and nights ahead.

FIVE

In the Forest

FROM the screened porch of a cottage set deep in the woods, much can be learned of the night activities of nearby animals. This vantage point is a compromise between indoors and out. Robert Louis Stevenson remarked that "Night is a dead monotonous period under a roof; but in the open it passes lightly . . . the hours are marked by changes in the face of Nature." The full effectiveness of darkness, however, should be felt by making one's bed in the forest itself. Beneath a great pine the needles of many seasons lie deep and resilient, a comfortable mattress where the tree itself shields away the dew.

To savor fully even a single summer night, the observation should begin just before sunset. The sunlight rapidly loses the burning dryness it has had all day. The shadow of a tree trunk seems damp and cool, like a breath from a waterfall.

The foliage overhead ceases its gentle agitation as the breeze dies, and disappearance of the fretful daytime brushing of leaf against leaf introduces into the woodland a noticeable hush. Everywhere there seems to be a counterpart of the wood wren which impressed W. H. Hudson: "that one fascinating sound would come to my ears from some distance away . . . little perlusive drops of musical sound, growing louder and falling away until they ran into one prolonged trill. . . . But . . . the bird is indefatigable and with his mysterious talk in the leaves would tire the sun himself and send him down the sky: for not until the sun has set and the wood has grown dark does the singing cease."

In the South, where the wild turkeys of America still run free, the gobblers strut and vocalize before the seemingly disinterested hen birds. Only the latter seem bent on filling their crops before the light fails. Then all of the turkeys will fly silently to their roosting places twenty or thirty feet above the ground. The darkening sky may silhouette them, their long, snake-like necks and conspicuous tails affording sure cues for identification.

In the north woods a clattering of claws on bark may draw attention to a gray squirrel or a red, hurrying from branch to branch on a devious aerial highway. A southern counterpart, the fox squirrel, may pause in running quietly from water oak to pine to tupelo, his long brush draping gracefully from the temporary perch. On a winter night these squirrels curl up securely in an insulated tree house built of leaves on some high limb. In summer they may cling simply, head up, to the trunk's rough bark, or crouch at the junction of bough and bole.

In either latitude, the last glint of day may pick up the pink nose and toes of an opossum climbing groundward for nocturnal foraging. Its gray fur is coarse—almost the color of Spanish moss. The strong, rat-like tail grips each support like a long tapering finger. As the animal progresses down the tree, its slow, deliberate movements contrast sharply with those of the active squirrels.

The opossum's strange hind feet have the middle three toes grouped together, the "small toe" somewhat by itself, and the "big toe" so large and thumb-like that it can be opposed to any of the other toes. As a result of having hands on the hind legs but not the fore, an opossum examines things with its rear feet. It uses them too to supplement the tail while clinging to branches and reaching out with pointed snout for such favorite fruit as persimmons, wild cherries, or blackberries.

If disturbed, this sole North American example of the marsupial (pouched) mammals may show its pointed teeth and hiss. Or it may suddenly "play 'possum" until danger disappears. In this trance-like state it lies on the ground with the body rolled on one side, the eyes closed, the tongue perhaps hanging from parted lips. The body muscles relax so thoroughly that if the animal is picked up by the tail, it hangs limply as though freshly dead. Even the heartbeat slows perceptibly.

As the opossum makes its twilight appearance and sleep

silences the day-active birds, a forest often becomes a concert hall for wood thrush and veery. The bold, disconnected phrasing of the wood thrush wells up within the sturdy, spotted-chested bird. Three or four flute-like notes, then a brief, soft trill, then silence. The singer sits motionless on an exposed branch, and the song reaches no certain finale. Always there is the promise of more. The veery's call seems disembodied, a spiral of continuous tone arising from the deep, damp shadows where the singer blends with the foliage. The song is a double chord, thin yet firm, that slides down the scale to die away, only to be followed by another graceful run, similar but slightly varied.

These good-night calls of the spotted thrushes are the most beautiful woodland music of all North America. Far different is the insistent, repetitious cry of "Whip—poor-will', Night—is-here', Night—is-here'" or the similar voicing of the chuck-will's widow in a southern forest. The cry may be almost deafening if the bird perches close by. But more often these refrains seem a lullaby, telling that the birds and beasts have accepted human presence or forgotten it for a few hours.

Cricket calls, like the voicings of thrush and whippoorwill and owl, appear to be a means whereby these animals stake out a breeding ground. Simultaneously they provide a claim to territory and a challenge to any invader of the same sex and kind. In tree crickets, territory claiming and mate summoning are combined in that they occur together. Yet each requires a separate mechanism. The only summons that our ears can discern is a shrill note, produced by the males, and heard by them through delicate "ears" just below the "knee" joint of their forelegs. But female tree crickets lack ears and are deaf. Still, when males raise their vibrating transparent wings to stridulate the persistent note, these deaf mates approach as though charmed by the sound. When they arrive,

however, the reason becomes clear. Each female nibbles greedily at a gland on the back of the male—a gland exposed whenever his wings are elevated into the "singing" position. His attraction lies in an odor emanating from this gland. For her the woods are silent but odorous, and she merely follows the aroma, testing the night air with her long sensitive antennae.

Frequently, on a night field trip, a person can approach a bush in which a tree cricket is shrilling his high-pitched note. Yet recognizing the direction from which the continuous sound arrives requires concentration. The insect is more than an inch long, and is scarcely disturbed by a searching flashlight, but its slender green body may be difficult to locate on a matching leaf. The late Dr. Frank E. Lutz, Curator of Insects and Spiders at the American Museum of Natural History, simplified this problem of cricket hunting by abandoning the usual way of trailing the singer. Dr. Lutz equipped himself with a physician's stethoscope. The cricket's song was loudest in *both* ears when the stethoscope's sensitive tip was directed toward the insect. Thus human ingenuity provided a substitute for the excellent sound-collecting funnels which cat or fox can turn toward a source of sound, or with which a deer or rabbit listens for the approach of danger.

Another insect follows an olfactory beam, hunting mice in the darkness. It is a black beetle, an inch or so in length, droning back and forth with bright orange hands emblazoned on its wing covers. No living mouse will draw it down, for the sexton beetle patrols the woods for signs of death. A mouse, a snake, a drying fish, a small bird's carcass—any of these merits attention from the insect. Anything larger must wait for other scavengers, for *Nicrophorus,* the sexton beetle, is a specialist.

Through the night air this insect employs a keen sense of

smell located in its outthrust knobbed antennae. A mouse need be dead only a few hours for *Nicrophorus* to find it. The beetle spirals to the ground close to the small carcass, then taxies in with wings folded—shoving and detouring through the grass jungle to reach the carrion. Once there the insect inspects the body by touch, rearing up on hind legs from every side, antennal knobs beating against the furry surface. Preliminaries over, the beetle performs a sudden turn and crawls under the carrion. *Nicrophorus'* back is down, its feet against the fur. Under and out on the other side; back below in another direction. Each move shows the powerful leverage in the black legs. The whole carcass rises to let the insect squeeze below.

Observers often feel dismayed at the next step *Nicrophorus* takes. It leaves the prize abruptly, and explores the surrounding land. For several feet it may rush away, only to circuit back again and repeat its inspection of the carrion. At several sites the beetle starts to dig, using its strong forelegs and butting head to push below the soil. Working its own body as a plow, it loosens the soil particles. Then back to the mouse's carcass, and away to plow some more.

At last the beetle appears satisfied and progress becomes more consecutive. From the side nearest the patch of plowed soil it moves under the carrion. This time the insect makes slow progress. But heave after heave shifts the carcass in the desired direction. Emerging at the far end, the insect hurries around and repeats the feat. In three such passes the mouse may have moved an inch. Away the beetle goes to the

softened soil, digging into it, loosening the particles to still greater depths and larger area. Back to the mouse for several further passes—heaving it from below, always toward the region of opened ground. Hour after hour this work continues.

A second beetle may join the task. If it is of the same sex there is a brief battle and the loser hastens off. But if the second beetle is of unlike sex, a pair has been established. Without courtship or other preliminaries, they work together. The carcass shifts a little faster. Sometimes one of a pair will remain at the body to move it in the dark, while the other works the soil at the burial site.

Obstacles may block the way. Each is examined, chewed through, forced aside, or detoured. Eventually the body reaches the plowed ground. There the same technique continues but with new effect. Each shuttling of the insects pushes earth from below the carcass, sinking it farther. Long before dawn the soil is level, the mouse several inches below the surface. There the pair is still in attendance, opening out the chamber one beetle-thickness larger than the carrion on all sides. They work the body into a ball, as a food supply for beetle grubs which will hatch in a few days from eggs the female *Nicrophorus* is already laying in the chamber.

Still the parents do not leave. Instead they feed and rest, waiting to nourish their new-hatched young by regurgitation. They will feed the grubs through their rapid growing period and provide in the nearby soil a tunnel in which each mature offspring can transform into another adult insect. Only then do the parents burrow upward to the open air, to repeat the process wherever each can find another carcass and another mate.

Along the ground and up the trunks of trees, darkness brings other insects a welcome respite from attacks by birds. Throughout the night in midsummer, brown shiny-bodied nymphs of cicadas work their way from the soil where, for many years, they have fed on roots. Laboriously each makes its way to a bush or tree and climbs, often for several feet. There, anchored by six sharp toes, the insect bursts its skin as though a zipper had been slid open along the back. From the old case emerges a greenish white body, soft and wet, with widespread eyes and rapier beak. When its feet pull clear, they drag the whole creature forward and upward an inch or two, there to hang while pulsing abdominal movements drive blood into expanding wings, spreading them downward as glassy flat membranes patterned with forking veins. Slowly in the humid air of night, the body armor and flight equipment harden. The insect flexes them with newly active muscles. By dawn the cicada is ready to fly, to find a mate, to start another generation on its way. Tomorrow the woods will ring with cicada song, the shrill high-speed drumming that seems to match the heat.

Moths, too, cling, resting on the bark of trees. A golden reddish eyeshine may gleam from the trunk. On closer inspection the sparkle becomes two bulging eyes. If the flashlight is turned off, the gleam vanishes abruptly. But if light continues to reach the insect, the clear gold of the eyes grows dusky and then vanishes completely. Nor is any eyeshine detectable by day. The moth becomes adapted to either darkness or daylight by moving dark pigments in the eye—withdrawing them below the mirror layer to expose it in dim light, or extending them to hide the mirror by day and absorb stray light in the same way as does the black pigment in human eyes.

The forest forms a double haven for wild things. At dusk birds of the open fields fly to the topmost branches to spend the night in greater security. Cardinals and other seed-eaters find advantage in trees which otherwise would seem to shelter chiefly worm-eating woodpeckers and warblers, with

here and there an owl in a tree hole. But with the coming
of night other animals desert the woodlands to forage in
the fields and beside streams: deer and red foxes, striped
skunks and banded raccoons. For them the forest is sanctuary
by day. More food is available where the sun can ripen
grass seeds and other plant products attractive to mice and
insects. Deer graze on the vegetation directly. The meat-
eaters take it second hand.

The woods of America are home to both the familiar red
fox and the slightly smaller gray fox. The red may make its
den in the brushy border where the trees thin out. At night
it ventures into the fields in search of meat and vegetables—
food on which it thrives in most of the country except the
southeast. The gray fox is a more southern animal, and is the
only one of its tribe which commonly climbs trees. It may
clasp a trunk and "shin itself" up like a bear would do, then
clamber around among the branches or hide within the
foliage. This ruse is often successful as an escape from pursuing dogs, but it seems to be tried on many occasions when
no enemy is in sight. Seldom does a gray fox invade pasture
land or other open area. As a result its presence in a forest
may go undetected for many years.

Tree country shelters few cottontail rabbits. The traditional "bunny" is a creature of weedy grasslands and briar
patches. To a very different member of the rabbit family,
the snowshoe "rabbit" or varying hare, woodland is a proper
living place. These forest animals rarely venture into open
country. Each is born at an unpredictable moment, without

shelter, somewhere along its mother's pathway. The parent turns, eats the afterbirth, licks her baby clean, and continues on her way. The young hare is already well furred, with eyes open and long ears alert. It follows promptly wherever she leads, and waits patiently if another addition is made to the family five minutes later. At two weeks of age the diet of the youngster is varied enough so that weaning is easy. This independence is so successful that 30 per cent of each year-group of hares normally survive past their first birthday.

No creature of the north woods is more fleet of foot than the snowshoe "rabbit." Few range so short a distance from their place of birth. The average hare explores less than a hundred acres of land. Many probably venture fewer than a hundred yards from home. Even when hunted they circle repeatedly, to stay within the small area familiar to them. Beyond it they are lost.

In early evening and again toward dawn, each varying hare hops off to feed, following a maze of trails but moving slowly to pick over the mixed vegetation. As fall arrives, the coat color changes from brown to white according to some internal calendar. In spring the alteration is in the opposite direction, thus earning the animal its "varying" name, and matching it well to the leaf litter of summer and the snow of winter.

The size of the hind feet is responsible for the term "snow-shoe." The hind toes spread widely, producing distinctive tracks at any season of the year. Summer trails become well worn in snowy weather too; but since the hare also tunnels through drifts and finds refuge in these during daylight hours, the animal is far harder to locate in winter than on a summer night.

Only at night can mice be found abroad in any numbers. Some of them rarely venture beyond the forest borders. But in the deep shadows of night certain white-footed deer mice of the woodlands discover deserted summer camps and move in to build a winter home of mattress stuffing. Every year the episode may be repeated. Through the long summer days no deer mouse shows itself. A mouse trap set in the forest will catch one almost every night. For as soon as one member of the large local population vanishes, another moves in by a slight expansion of territory. Whether trap or owl, fox or panther was responsible for the disappearance makes little difference. Every night some mice are caught by predators. Few of them survive for more than a year. Only shyness and a prodigious rate of reproduction save them from extermination.

A night observer needs no flashlight to show a path through the forest. It is more fun to practice using the full capacity of the human senses. To feel the way, with every means available, is to recall Henry Thoreau's diary of his year at Walden: "It is darker in the woods, even in common nights, than most suppose. I frequently had to look up at the opening between the trees above the path in order to learn my route, and, where there was no cart-path, to feel with my feet the faint track which I had worn, or steer by the known relation of particular trees which I felt with my hands, passing between two pines for instance, not more than eighteen inches apart, in the midst of the woods, invariably, in the darkest night."

Like Thoreau, one risks an encounter with a skunk, for this nocturnal forager will yield no path to a quick-moving stranger. At the slow pace required by darkness in the forest, however, the skunk has time to choose a different route, and can pretty much be relied upon to do so. Its interest in the dark woods is related to the animal food it can find there. As much as three-quarters of the skunk's springtime diet is meadow mice, and it is amazingly nimble at catching an unwary rodent. By summer the shrews and white-footed mice of the forest floor are mere supplements to vast numbers of insects, especially crickets and beetles. Fruits which can be reached from the ground provide dessert, for the skunk varies its food selection widely, depending on what is available. It cannot climb, but digs many of its chosen delicacies from the soil and rotting logs.

In the forest darkness a person may stumble on a porcupine. Yet this well-armed rodent is more likely to be busy in a tree, stuffing itself with vegetation to be digested in daytime hours. Usually the woodland furnishes every need: leaves of fresh shrubs and herbs in springtime, foliage of cedar, pine, and hemlock at any season, and the nutritious inner bark of many kinds of trees. Clinging to a limb with all four legs and the special spines below the short blunt tail, a porcupine chips away the dead, dry outer bark, letting the flakes fall to the ground. Then, sitting on a branch or rearing up against the trunk, the animal chisels away at the soft tissues just outside the wood. Occasionally moonlight picks out these shining "blazes"—for they occur at any height above the ground, and range in size from a few inches in diameter to several feet high, almost girdling the trunk.

A more dangerous prowler in the night woods is a rattlesnake or copperhead. Such snakes can coil and strike without benefit of eyes, and snatch a small victim to quick death. Between eye and nostril on each side, all pit vipers bear a conical depression lined with sensitive cells. These are like twin radar antennae, responding to radiant energy of the thermal type. Each pit keeps the snake informed of any local warmth or chill. When both are stimulated simultaneously, their overlapping fields of sensitivity have centered just ahead on some object which may provide the snake a dinner in the dark.

A stepped-on viper gives no buzz of warning; but neither

does it have much chance to coil and strike full length, so that boots and jeans should give adequate protection. Because of man's size and height, moreover, he is safer than the small birds sleeping in low bushes or the mice feeding on the ground. These, like wet-bodied frogs, have body temperatures quite unlike those of the surrounding soil and foliage. The evaporation of moisture from frog skin keeps them cool. Birds and mammals maintain a high and constant body heat. It is these differences which the night-active vipers seek, without need for light.

If the forest roof is slightly open, an occasional star is visible through the foliage. Toward midnight a light breeze may spring up, and the stars wink fitfully through the moving leaves. Among the oaks the air seems to mutter as tough blade bumps blade, like leather against leather. Willow leaves whisper. Poplars prattle furiously. Each tree type has a distinctive conversation with the wind. The breeze "fans in the maple, harps in the needles of a pine, sighs in silver birches, and rolls like an organ in the cedar." By day it is easy to identify the trees according to bark and branching, by arrangement and shape of leaves. By night their boles look much alike. It is their sounds which are most distinctive.

In the night wind, each tree seems to wave its high branches slowly, the leisurely movement in keeping with the long-term nature of a tree's life. By contrast, animal affairs are transient indeed. Many mice have not survived the night. God alone, who sees the sparrow fall, knows how many generations of owls and foxes have come and gone since the trees were seedlings. Only the stars seem fixed. Somehow the cold light from outer space, which started on its way hundreds or thousands of years ago, has a reassuring quality. "Give any man a star on which he can fix his eye and he can reach as far as his imagination points the way."

SIX

Echoes of the Night

EXACTLY when bats appeared to enliven the night is still unknown. But the stage for their coming was set by events some hundred million years ago.

Insects became more numerous and diversified. Great numbers took to daytime immobility, escaping in this way from detection by prowling amphibians and lizards, and the big-eyed dragonflies in the sky above. Instead the day-sleepers flew by night. The night-fliers winged their way to potential mates by scent and sound alone. Katydids and mayflies, stoneflies and caddis, gnats and moths of a thousand kinds, filled the Mesozoic night with their flutterings. For thousands, perhaps millions of years, they seem to have had the night air to themselves. Below them the dinosaurs came and went. A few of these reptiles took to the air. But neither bird nor bat hunted the insects flying through the starlit skies.

Homes for bats made an appearance along with the dinosaurs. The giant ferns and club mosses of the coal ages were gone. The needle-leaved conifers were declining. Gradually the broad-leaved trees spread over the Mesozoic land, providing canopies under which a bat could hide, and hollow trunks enclosing a daytime remnant of the night.

The stage was set, yet a gap of some twenty million years in the fossil record hides the detailed transformation to more modern life. Into this void the dinosaurs vanished without a trace. Bats appeared among the dwellers of the Eocene. Their skeletons were so similar to the bony support of current kinds that their habits must have been about the same. Like modern bats in style of flight, they surely depended upon sonar ranging to dodge obstacles at night and to find their insect prey. No longer were the nocturnal insect swarms safe on their journeys through the dark. They afforded ample food supply to the furry little mammals which developed rubbery webbing between elongated fingers. With exquisite control the bats flapped in fast pursuit.

Insects to catch at night, trees to hide in by day—these alone the bats required. In the fifty million years since bats appeared, no other night-flying creatures have contested seriously their claim to the insect hordes. When birds arose, a few assumed the habits of nighthawk and whippoorwill. They trawled through the skies with mouths agape, swallowing whatever insect blundered into the open trap. Bats alone chase down their victims one by one. With staccato calls at ultrasonic pitches echoing back to their ears, they detect food and distinguish it from obstacles that bar their flight.

The ultrasonic echoing of bats serves them well for winged navigation in dim light and for finding havens for the day. Continued night is the special seclusion a bat cries for at dawn. A hollow tree, a hole in the ground, a niche in a building, are all alike in this respect. Methodically the bats search out all natural caves, neglected mine tunnels, belfries, attic crannies—even the gaps a careless carpenter leaves when readying a roof for shingles. These are the nooks into which both night and bats retreat together when dawn spreads across the sky.

It is curious that an animal having so few living enemies should have chosen as sleeping sites so many temporary shelters. By the time a tree affords space to bats, its rotted trunk is about ready to crash to earth. An attic or belfry that men regard lightly enough to permit bats to live there is usually part of a building which should be condemned, one about to tumble down from the infirmities of age. Mine tunnels collapse when their untended timbers molder and decay. And in the long view of the fossil record, even the tree way of life seems to be in decline. By the Eocene, when bat remains were first preserved, the earliest grasses and prairies had begun to replace forests, taking over land with hollow trees and foliage which could hide a bat.

Nor are the daytime shadows into which the flying mammals creep all alike in suitability. An attic or a solitary tree may grow too hot in summer sun. Winter's cold and winds reach into exposed crannies, and steal away a sleeping bat's heat until life itself is threatened. The broad-leaved trees stand gaunt and batless through winter and into spring. Caves may be remote from food supplies. Only a mine tunnel affords a natural seclusion in regions of igneous rocks, where water-dissolved caves are absent altogether. Yet for the little "companions of the dark," a cave or mine tunnel offers one special attraction: night and day in every month its temperature remains about the same. Accurately it averages the year's gain and loss of heat at every hour. This gives the bats some choice: cooler caves for winter use, and warmer ones as nurseries. Any cave with a temperature above the freezing point will do for the day.

Bats chase their insect prey only at night. All their feeding is air-borne. And when the cooler days of fall seriously reduce the food supply, some kinds of bats fly through the night to southern lands, migrating with the birds to compete with populations in the tropics for insects. Most northern bats sleep out the winter in hibernation, hanging motionless in some deep dark cavern, filed away until next years' spring.

An autumn bat is stocked with fat, enough to last a winter. If foodless days from fall to spring do not demand more energy than the store of fat can yield, the hibernating mammal will survive. By drastic lowering of the body temperature, all chemical activity slows to match the energy supply on hand. The bat's blood heat falls to a fraction of a degree above that of the roosting site. If the cave is too warm, chemical activity continues at too high a rate and the bat will starve. If the wintering place chills down to the freezing point, the bat may die of cold. These two extremes are the biggest enemies a bat must face. Winter is the ebb tide of its life.

Even in a perfect hibernating site the flying mammal does not sleep in continuous torpor. At intervals each awakens, elevates its body temperature to normal summer range, flits back and forth until its wings are stretched completely, then settles down again for another week or two of slowed heart-beat and intermittent breathing.

The reproductive activities of the flying mammals are almost entirely restricted to their roosting sites. The females give birth to their young shortly after the hibernating period has reached its end—usually one baby to each mother. At first they are naked, clinging things that clamber in their mother's fur, and hold tight to a nourishing nipple. The parent may fly forth at night to catch her stomach full of insects—still with the baby holding on.

At last she leaves it at home—clinging to the wall or roof until she returns. The youngsters greet their mothers with high-pitched voices the parents recognize. Even if a baby has scrambled to a new location, the adult bat seeks out her own, to pick it up against her breast and feed. Then, after about a month, the young reach flying size, and venture forth with the parents to feed themselves on living insect prey. On this first night in the dark world above, young males and females are there in equal numbers. Each dawn

the returning bats are fewer and more predominantly females, since the males soon drift off to find solitary homes.
Before long, the nursery has females only, and continues so
through summer, fall, and winter hibernation.

Winter is hardest on the solitary males, but those that
survive make use of waking nighttime hours whenever the
outdoor weather is warm enough to venture forth. They hunt
out the nursery colonies of females, and visit one torpid mate
after another until their virility is spent. A dozen times in a
winter the colony may receive these soft-winged callers. By
early spring every female is pregnant.

A fresh brood of young has been assured. Their birthdates
come close together, usually within a week or so, although
the impregnations were scattered throughout the hibernating months. For a female bat can store and sustain the living
sperm cells the male provides, until her eggs are ready to
receive them. Older bats reach this stage a few days earlier
than the one-year-olds, so that the young of more mature
mothers arrive about a week before those of bats born the
previous year.

To this extent, the continuous night of caves can be said
to supply a "nest" for bats. One other warm-blooded creature shows this same interest in the lightless depths of the
earth. The oil bird, *Steatornis,* of Trinidad and Venezuela
(known to the local people as a "guachero") makes use of
caverns to rear its young, and flies out at night to feed on
fruits. Like the bat, the oil bird uses sonar echo-location to
find its way around. Although the bird's cries are brief—one

to two thousandths of a second—like those of the flying mammal, the pitch is low enough for a man to hear. The cave-filling din averages 7,000 cycles, between four and five octaves above middle C. And like the bat, the bird cannot find its way around if either ears or voice are stopped. Both bat and bird use versions of the blind man's cane, tapping to produce a sound which can echo back from obstacles in the path. Since sound in air travels about a foot per thousandth of a second, the brief call or tap is completed in time for an echo to be heard separately. A longer cry would overlap and conceal the repercussion.

The naturalist Alexander von Humboldt, who first drew scientists' attention to the oil birds' nesting place, told of a forest of white shoots as much as two feet high, deep in the cave near Caripe, Venezuela. This is the outcome of seeds dropped by the birds. A wealth of seedlings grow straight upward without the light that would cause them to bend in any direction. Year after year these frustrated young plants grow tall and die in the cavern's continual night, each having done its best with the foodstuffs stored within the seed, and with the rich guano on the cave floor underneath the roosting birds.

Of all the places in the world where animals congregate, none has so black and continuous a night as a cave. For this reason alone, the caverns offer a lasting haven for animals that shun the sun. Into caves have crept a strange assortment, as company for the bats. Many of these animals are white, through lack of pigment. In a lighted place each would be

conspicuous enough to invite attack, but below the surface of the earth, they borrow blackness from their surroundings, and shed their handicap. Many lack eyes, or have these sense organs so reduced that competition in daylight leaves them far behind eye-bearing kinds in the race for survival. In perpetual night, the animal with good eyes is the one at a disadvantage, since its nervous system is attuned to dependence on vision and relative neglect of the other senses. Scientists still debate whether animals with degenerate eyes adopted caves, or whether continued restriction to niches in total darkness led to a loss of vision. But cavern life the world over is famous not only for its bats but also for its eyeless fish, sightless salamanders, blind crustaceans, beetles, and flatworms.

In the perpetual darkness that surrounds them, cave animals are in constant danger from one another. Most of them are opportunistic meat-eaters, ready to snatch any meal that comes their way. In subterranean ponds and streams, touch and taste take the place of vision. Cave crayfish and camel crickets have feelers extended enormously, often exceeding the body in length. Legs may be thickly set with long hairs, increasing the likelihood that touch will be stimulated in time to detect prey or enemies. The water may carry dissolved chemicals in both directions—toward a predator which can detect the flavor of a potential victim, and toward a lesser creature whose sense of taste may warn it of an enemy's approach. Some of the swimming crustaceans bear extraordinarily large organs of chemical sense, serving them much as taste buds do a human tongue, keeping them continually apprised of neighbors in the dark depths.

Some cave animals are extremely sensitive to any rise in temperature. The crustacean *Niphargus* dies if warmed to a mere 68 degrees F., and apparently avoids warmer air, remaining in the darkness of underground retreats.

Most of the continuous inhabitants of caves are small. Perhaps their size matches the food supply, since in a cave there are no green plants, no sun energy that they could trap by day. The food in a cavern must enter from the outside. Sometimes it comes as a tree root, pushing through the porous soil and spreading out along the walls and ceiling of a grotto. Sometimes it arrives as microscopic algae, suspended in the stream which still cuts through the tortuous passageways. Bats, returning from a night-long hunt for insects, come burdened with a fare so rich in nitrogen that their digestive systems cannot extract it all. The residue falls to the cave floor as a dark guano, valuable commercially for fertilizer, and useful as a source of the niter for making gunpowder. Molds extract from the bat manure many substances that they need for energy and growth. Insects feed on the molds, taking at third hand the nourishment the bats brought in from the night sky. Cave centipedes and spiders catch the insects, and once more the energy is passed along.

One type of insect takes its food in the cave more directly. This flattened wingless creature steals blood from sleeping bats. It is the black "batbug," close relative of the bedbug. Indeed, it seems clear that man's early use of caves for homes gave him an opportunity to inherit from bats one of their normal parasites. Perhaps man drove the bats from the caves he wished to occupy, and the wingless hungry followers remained behind—to starve unless they could change their hosts. Man's blood proved just as nourishing, and *Cimex* adopted him.

Other denizens of the caves are more like men; they enter only far enough to escape from the outside world. Snake and skunk, bear and bobcat choose these shelters as a place to sleep. For them a dry cave is best. To true cave animals, dryness means death from lack of food. Around them the rainless room must have a humidity that is high and constant. The roof should drip and moisture film the walls, since this extract of the soil above is rich in dissolved and suspended materials. Colloidal matter of plant origin comes down with the limy salts. The latter precipitate as incrustations: flowstone, helictites, stalactites, and stalagmites. Yet even as the water vaporizes into the cave's high humidity, leaving behind these solid monuments, mites and springtails crowd to the unseen water's edge to browse and suck nourishment. Fungi thrive on the same colloidal food, and support small numbers of snails and fungus-eating beetles. Even on the woody roots of trees, plant lice may find an underground home.

Exploring the eternal darkness of a cave can furnish all manner of adventure. With no natural light to help, a torch or flashlamp is almost indispensable. Provident spelunkers carry two, one as a spare in case the other fails. Creeping and scrambling, they follow passageways carved by underground streams that may have flowed unsuspected for centuries. Often the corridor divides and each division narrows down until a full-grown man can barely wriggle through to another room. The arched ceiling may be bare and lifeless. Sometimes it bears a quivering velvet of close-packed pendant bats. More often the bats form islands of blackish brown: here a patch of little ones; there a clump of big ones. Each species clusters only with its own kind. Even the sexes choose separate roosting places.

Close at hand the flashlamp's beam encircles a three-inch slender salamander clinging to the wall, peering with bulging eyes into the unfamiliar radiance. On the roof above, two pale brown shining bodies hang from a single spot, and from each to the other, soft-looking appendages are festooned in exquisite grace. At last an insect has been found to bear sixteen legs! Or so it appears. Then the camel cricket—for such it is—lowers her body still more out of a lengthwise slit in the hollow skin. Daintily she steps from the six hip boots still clinging to the roof, and from the long glove fingers of her former self slips her two tremendous feelers. She waves them back and forth in search of danger, while her pulsing abdomen shortens and adjusts itself to the new load at its tip—an egg-laying scimitar with which she will eventually thrust her eggs deep into the muddy floor. Two insects now— one pulsing with life, the other an empty shell. Six legs for each plus a pair of feelers—a total of sixteen appendages.

To watch events normally transpiring in total darkness, it is important to move the light beam as seldom as possible, to produce no sudden sounds or gusts of air. Many of the insects, whether blind or with eyes (as in camel crickets), are acutely sensitive to movements of the air around them.

Quiet is requested of all visitors to the Waitomo caverns two hundred miles north of Wellington, New Zealand, in the only caves in the world that contain luminescent animals. Here the maggots of mosquito-sized flies produce a world-famous and unique display. As they cling to the ceiling of each grotto, they gleam with a continuous blue-green light carried on the tail segment. Below them they let down beaded pendulums—threads as much as two feet long, secreted from their mouths. Each thread bears mucous globules at intervals. Other flies and midges bump into these sticky threads, are captured and struggle to escape. The thread spinner then swallows thread and victim—like an angler reeling in his line. How much the luminescence affects the catch is unknown. But if a visitor raises his voice, the threads appear to serve each maggot as a microphone, and the vibrations transmitted to it are enough to induce a complete blackout.

Reverberating sound or flashing light is enough to excite a bat as it hangs from the vaulted roof. And any prolonged disturbance of the roosting place leads often to a mass evacuation. If the entire colony is found in an alternate location and disturbed again, it may shift to a third site or back to the first. Concerted movements such as these suggest both that bats communicate with one another and that the colony includes leaders familiar with several strongholds.

In the millions of years since bats began their nocturnal forays in search of flying insects, the plants and animals have changed a lot. Cave kinds, in their perpetual night, have been less affected by the progress of time and for them conservatism has become a way of life. But the advent of men has meant more than occasional interference with subterranean passageways, to make a primitive home, or to build an attraction for the tourist dollar. Deserted mine tunnels, damp basements, or vacant attics do not compensate the lesser creatures for these invasions of their age-old privacy; mankind's effect reaches beyond anything we can repay.

Within a few miles of Mammoth Cave National Park is the town of Horse Cave, Kentucky. The cavern for which the settlement was named provided entertainment for visitors and income for its owners until World War II. Paved paths, electric lights, insecticide bombs, and drainage systems made the tour pleasant and safe. Patrons even enjoyed a boat ride on the subterranean Lost River. But during the years when tourism suffered from the gasoline shortage, an increase in local population led to a wider use of Lost River as a sewer. Nowhere in town were septic tanks needed. All a householder had to do was dig through the soil until he found a crevice in the underlying rock, and lead his house discharge to this point. By 1946 the odor in Horse Cave became so nauseating that the cavern's value as a tourist attraction reached zero. The blind fish and eyeless crayfish which had survived in numbers within the cave could no longer be found without a special trip up Lost River to a point above the sewage area. Living conditions for creatures in the dark deteriorated beyond their endurance. Townspeople knew, of course, why the cave was closed and no longer brought visitors to their region. But community conscience too, went down the free drainage system into "the biggest natural sewer in all the world."

In this area of Kentucky, the pendulum has swung to exactly opposite the point where man came in. How far this situation is from former days, when caverns were highly prized by primitive men as retreats from the winter's cold and the summer's heat, from savage beasts that could be kept from the barricaded door! Then men swept their floors and buried their dead in caves, where the bodies would dry, be mummified or reduced to skeletons. Man's artistic sense led him to erect crude scaffoldings, and to crouch there facing a wetted wall or ceiling while blowing onto its surface ground rock of many colors through fine grass stems. This was the first airbrush illustration, and some of the finest known. In Spain and France this cave decoration dates from prehistoric days. Yet, except for some Oriental panoramic art, it shows a closer observation of animals in motion than developed again until the camera was invented.

Man's use of caves has changed, but bats still seek them as dark havens before dawn. The bats continue to fly in the same erratic way, able to stop or go, to turn and twist, in ways no bird can imitate. No bat has learned to soar, perhaps because night affords few upward currents of air to make soaring possible. More likely a slow gliding path has advantages only by day, when a visual search for food can be detailed in good light. Under the stars or even the moon, no flying mammal with eyes the size of those in northern bats could see to find food on the ground below. Sonar ranging takes the place of eyes and helps the bats again at twilight to locate a home deep in the earth. There daytime is dark-time, like an echo of the night just past and a sample of the one to follow.

SEVEN

In the City

When a man winds the clock, puts out the cat, and locks the door for the night, he feels secure. As Thoreau put it: "The witches are all hung, and Christianity and candles have been introduced." Broadway seems deserted. The pinioned ducks in the park's artificial lake gabble quietly. Like the penned deer chewing their cuds, the birds are fat from day-time handouts—peanuts, popcorn, chewing gum, sandwiches. Pigeons from the city square and vulgar starlings squat silently on cornice and window ledge. The sparrows are asleep on high shrubs. Gray squirrels take their rest in tree holes or between the trunk and some big limb.

The metropolis appears under perfect control. Each inhabitant of the carefully tended human hive has his own place to spend the dark hours. Even the pets are fully provided for. Budgies and canaries are safe in their cages. The dog's leash hangs behind the door, and he is probably dreaming audibly on his pillow in a corner of the room.

Any wild creature abroad would seem an exception. Yet in the heart of a great metropolis, many are to be found. Two hundred and twenty different kinds of birds have been recorded flying freely in New York's Central Park. Most of these arrived and left by night. The census for the entire metropolitan area is now above 350 species. No doubt some of them were oceanic birds blown in by on-shore gales. But for the majority, night brings them through the city every year simply because Manhattan is at the junction point of two migration routes—the Hudson River valley and the New England coastal flyway. Their migrating habits were well established long before Christopher Columbus and Henry Hudson. So far the skyscrapers have not forced them to change their course.

Often the city dweller sleeps through the passage of the flocks. Aldo Leopold commented that he "once knew an educated lady, banded by Phi Beta Kappa, who told me that she had never heard or seen the geese that twice a year proclaim the revolving seasons to her well-insulated roof." Still they arrow overhead or settle for a rest on an open stretch of water. It may be Boston's Jamaica Pond or Chicago's frontage on Lake Michigan. For years the zoo in Bronx Park has displayed a fine gander and half a dozen of his flock, trapped during night migration and cared for so well that the young of the flock were reared in captivity year after year.

Just a few trees, grouped in a back yard or a park, will attract crows in winter and hawks in spring or fall. At sunset the crows come in from surrounding land, and with clamor silhouette themselves against the sky as they wheel and settle, boil upward and come back again. Of the hawks, the rough-legged flies later in the day than most, and is often mistaken for an owl when it approaches the nightly roosting place. Sometimes the hawk seems reluctant to reveal its chosen spot. It waits on a fence or telephone pole until dusk hides the final flight into its favorite tree.

A city park that includes streams and pools affords an oasis for wildlife—even some of the larger mammals. Not long ago a groundhog made a burrow in a lawn on Riverside Drive. A fox found a space for a den under the grandstand at the Yankee Stadium. A colony of muskrats lives in the New York Botanic Gardens.

These same gardens furnish the shrubs used every night by countless English sparrows. Thousands more of these birds know where houses have a sheltering niche. Along the waterways of Bronx Park, cattails and reeds are nocturnal havens from wind for juncoes and tree sparrows, swallows and occasional cardinals. The waterways are nesting areas for red-winged blackbirds and still more muskrats. Tall trees provide safe perches for herons. Flickers cling to the trunks. Any knothole big enough for a mouse offers a bedroom to a chickadee or a nuthatch.

Occasionally a nocturnal animal is discovered and reported in the newspaper. William Beebe tells of trapping "eleven magnificent mink on the Bronx River in the Zoological Park, well within the city's boundaries"; of a wild bear captured beside one of New York's nearer reservoirs of fresh water; and of nightly dam-building by beavers within thirty miles of Manhattan—engineering so skilful that to save roads and dwellings from the spreading ponds it became necessary to trap and "relocate" the fur-bearers.

Less than five blocks south of Miami's main shopping and theater street, route U.S. 1 crosses a metal drawbridge. Under that span wild manatees collect each night and remain long enough after dawn to excite a visitor who comes upon a real sea-cow—the mermaid of ancient mariners—perhaps nursing her calf while clasping it womanlike with a broad flipper.

The "most nocturnal mammal," the flying squirrel, often finds a home in the city, taking advantage of trees along the avenue or on the green squares. Any park is a good place to watch for these creatures a few hours after sunset. A soft churring sound is their chief call. A tree-hole affords a suitable habitation. In the spill of a night light, a flying squirrel may be seen scampering up a tree trunk, leaping off with four legs stiffly spread. On stretched membranes it may plane thirty feet or more to reach another tree. At the critical moment it flicks its tail and alights head up, ready to climb rapidly for another takeoff. These rodents commonly frolic in tandem—guiding their glides with a flattened furry tail as long as the chipmunk-sized body. At times they freeze motionless for fifteen or twenty minutes at a stretch, without even a twitch of the long black whiskers. By dawn they have vanished again, to sleep the clock around and more, often

four or five together in a fiber-lined cavity no bigger than a man's coat pocket.

Flying squirrels are fond of fruits and nuts, but enticing them to a window sill for closer acquaintance requires both skill and luck. The shelf must be at a level to which they can leap from a tree and then away again, for unlike bats, these nocturnal midget squirrels can only glide, not flap or fly. At times they do visit feeding stations built for the daytime birds. They will clean up a little pile of dry rolled oats—relishing them as a delicacy preferable to sunflower seeds or apple.

Feeding the night-active birds is much more difficult. An

owl is unlikely to find scraps of meat, and providing insects for nighthawk or whippoorwill is not feasible since these birds feed on the wing. But nesting boxes for owls can be highly successful, since hollow trees and similar hideaways are hard to find within city limits—dead wood is so regularly pruned away. A nest is not a home except for owls. Swallows and bluebirds, robins and woodpeckers use birdboxes only during their breeding seasons, and stay in them at night solely when eggs must be incubated or nestlings kept from cold. An owl sleeps inside, however, and if the home box is successful, man has rewarded an ally in his struggle to keep the vicinity free of rats and mice. The quavering call of the owl at eventide is an extra dividend.

No special bait is required to draw night-flying insects to a city. They flock to artificial lights. Moths of all sizes arrive, from the "micros" with eighth-inch wing expanse—adults of the tiny caterpillars that excavate narrow, serpentine mines within the thin green of an oak leaf—to the giant silk-worm moths that are the delight of all who find them. Brown moths and green moths, striped ones and types with black polka dots on an ash-gray wing, all of them settle facing the illumination, like a Muslim throng bending low toward the dawn.

On no two nights will the population of light-worshippers be the same. In their respective seasons there will be golden-eyed lacewing flies, and the heavy-bodied chafers known as "May beetles" or "June bugs" according to the month of their activity. On any summer night mayflies can emerge from a river or lake in such enormous numbers that they sweep over the city like a blizzard. Their delicate bodies are fitted for a brief life, and below each street lamp, under every store window, in all corners protected from the wind, dawn may find their corpses heaped to a depth of a foot or more.

Stoneflies and caddisflies sometimes throng to lights in numbers almost as great as the mayfly swarms. But these sudden deluges are usually brief and distract us from the tremendous variety arriving one by one on "ordinary" nights. To obtain samples from the insect population, scientists often set up a special trap, consisting of a powerful lamp bulb burning above a metal funnel leading into a collecting jar charged with lethal gas. Moths rush to the light, fall through the funnel, and remain to be gathered in the morning. One summer-long study of this kind ended with nearly 13,000 individuals captured by three traps, and then classified. Six hundred and sixty species were represented. Of these, 50 were so common as to account for all but 15 per cent of the total. The rest of the catch—the 610 species—came in ones and twos, and the average number barely reached three!

The color of each light influences the numbers and kinds of insects attracted. A few years ago, residents of Schenectady saw a row of nine trap lamps erected at the General Electric Laboratories. Each was of a different color, and from the catch below each bulb, the experimenters learned which hue was most attractive, which least, to the nocturnal insect visitors. The blue end of the spectrum drew the largest number; it contains the energy most stimulating to an insect's eye. Red lured the fewest; red is invisible altogether to many insects and hence equivalent to no light at all. Soon a compromise was reached. New bulbs were marketed, yellow as a daffodil, to throw a light bright enough for human eyes without attracting more than small numbers of night-flying insects. But to the city's blue neon signs and white-lit windows, both people and insects are strongly drawn.

In darkness a wide variety of insect life is on the wing. It is like taking part in a living detective story to sit quietly in the outdoor dark, trying to identify each animal that moves. Fluttering wraiths give off a soft whirr as they hover around a flowering shrub. In daylight they are sleepy moths. At night they take over the errands of hummingbirds. They tend the flowers and pollinate many kinds that are shut when bees and birds are active. The sound of moth wings is quite different from that of the "shard-borne beetle with his drowsy hums." Chafers have a harshness in their buzzing, and they blunder into foliage or tumble clownlike to the ground when they attempt to settle on a plant.

On warm nights human noses, too, can record the varied scents of flowers. You can close your eyes and walk twenty feet right to a honeysuckle bush. Petunias hoard, then pour forth, their fragrance in darkness. But all of these scents depend upon a generous residue of warmth left from the sunlight of the previous day. If the night is chill, the plants hold back. Few insects would venture forth to pollinate their blossoms.

Some of the odors attracting insects through the city night come from other insects. An easy way to show this reliance on scent is to cage a female of any of the spectacular moths— a huge cecropia, a pale green luna, a polyphemus, or a promethia. No matter how battered her wings, she will loose into the night air a potent fragrance detected by males of her kind. They will fly toward her at top speed; marked specimens have traveled more than six miles through the darkness.

The patient French naturalist Jean Henri Fabre made an elaborate study of this night-odorous habit. For eight evenings, to a captive female emporer—the Great Peacock— came the largest of all European moths. "They followed the direction of the wind; not one flew against it. . . . The total of [male moths] attracted on these eight nights amounted to a hundred and fifty; a stupendous number when I consider what searches I had to undertake during the two following years. . . . Cocoons of the Great Peacock are at least extremely rare, as the trees on which they are found are not common."

This demonstration can be repeated in any city. By early morning one or more male moths will find even a single open window in a house where a female of their kind has emerged from her cocoon, and beat their wings against the screen. Once admitted they will fly straight to the spot she occupies. But an observer who cares to try an experiment can prove to himself how completely the males depend upon the female's scent. If she is transferred to a tight glass or plastic enclosure, they will pay no attention to her big fluttering wings. Instead they seek only the place where she was last free in the room. A bit of absorbent tissue over which the female has crept is more attractive to them than a live (and willing) mate whose scent glands have been removed.

Other courtships are visible in city darkness as momentary points of light. A century ago, the great experimental physicist Michael Faraday wrote to his mother from the European continent: "Tell B. I have crossed the Alps and the Apennines; I have been at the Jardin des Plantes; at the museum arranged by Buffon; at the Louvre, among the *chefs-d'oeuvre* of sculpture and the masterpieces of paintings; at the Luxembourg palace, amongst Rubens' works; that I have seen a GLOW WORM! ! !"

A glow-worm can be found in almost any city garden, vacant lot, or park. Wherever fallen leaves and rotting wood accumulate, these insects search out smaller creatures they can subdue and eat. Usually a glow-worm proves to be the wingless female of a special firefly, *Phengodes*. In the dark it shines with rows of bright points along the sides of its

three-quarter-inch length. Smaller and less spectacular fac-
similes turn out to be the immature stages of other kinds of
fireflies. Like the winged males which flash their tail lamps
while flying over the lawn among the shrubbery, the adult
glow-worms shine their lights and attract a mate. Why the
young of "lightning bugs" should bear luminous spots remains a mystery.

Sometimes in a humid summer evening, city children catch
fireflies by the dozens and enclose them in a bottle. The collec-
tive light output of the seething throng makes it possible to
read newsprint held close. Baltimore children are paid to
collect fireflies for science, to be studied by the thousand at
the Johns Hopkins University in an attempt to fathom their
engineering secret of cool illumination.

In some Oriental cities, a well appointed summer party on
the lawn will have fireflies in abundance. For the guests' delight, the host may send to the market for a few hundred of
the insects. Servants release them at intervals so that the
streaks of harmless fire will liven up the scene. And this
enjoyment of insects is in keeping with Buddhist beliefs,
since it does them no harm.

Each year the Academy of Natural Sciences in Philadelphia
sends out invitations to another kind of party. When springtime reaches the proper stage, postcards go through the
mails announcing a night field trip to one of the city's parks.
"Bring flashlights." And citizens, young and old, gather by
the dozens to hear a choir and watch the singers. Each chor-
ister perches in a pond or a well-controlled Park Department

stream and strums his vocal cords with air blown from lungs to throat sacs and back. Frogs and toads provide the music. The fossil record suggests that their tune has been the same for 200 million years—an antiquity greater than that of any other wind instrument. By comparison, the songs of birds and the calls of mammals seem the preliminary tuning of an upstart orchestra.

A city field trip in the night *should* be held each autumn to draw attention to the climax of cricket chirps and grasshopper stridulation. In nature's orchestra, this is the percussion section. Its lineage extends even farther back than that of frogs and toads. From tree and bush and goldenrod the insects beat out a hundred tempos in as many keys.

The commonest of these chirping sounds comes from the fat black crickets creeping through the tangled grass. Their calls come so regularly through the bedroom window that men have timed them. Temperature adjusts the rate. Two chirps per second at 70 degrees; one chirp each second at 55. Count the chirps in fifteen seconds, add forty and you have the temperature. The warmer the night, the merrier the grig!

The calls of insects have attracted attention for countless years. A fad for caging crickets has sprung up many times— in China, Japan, Greece, Italy, southern France, Portugal, and in Portuguese-speaking Brazil. In the eighth century A.D., upon the approach of fall the ladies of the Chinese court placed captive crickets in small golden cages, and kept them near their pillows to relieve the monotony of lengthening nights. The idea spread, until a cricket cult claimed members throughout the country. Some crickets were prized for fighting ability, others for their stridulated song. Elaborate homes and special utensils were constructed to house and care for the insects. People became connoisseurs, comparing and rating the songs of individual crickets. But only in Japan did city-dwellers make it a custom to go outdoors on autumn nights for the sole purpose of listening to crickets. This pastime too died out. It was simpler to have country people collect the insects and sell them caged at the public market.

Cricket calls after dark in a city mean that the impoverished soil has supported enough plants to feed the insect to maturity. Only the adults make the sound. They scavenge through the blackness, taking advantage of a wide range of foods. In turn, they are fair game to larger creatures such as toads and skunks, that patrol the night and disappear at dawn into niches no one knows. Ordinarily these lives dovetail with those of men, fitting together so easily that few people know how many animals retain their wildness within the city's limits. Each makes use of metropolitan space for a chosen period in every twenty-four hours.

Major scientific discoveries have been made in a city garden, during the darkness before dawn. Jan E. Purkinje slept so poorly that he arose in the night and wandered out among his flowers. Underneath the starlit sky his eyes could see no colors, but with nose and fingers he explored the blossoms to tell larkspur from columbine, primrose from

99

nicotine, gentian from iris. Strange, he thought, how bright the blue flowers seem! By day the yellows and reds claim attention first. At night they're far darker. Could it be that human eyes change when light intensity grows less?

Later, in his darkened laboratory, Purkinje projected on a wall a spectrum spread from sunlight by a prism. Which part is brightest? The greenish yellow, certainly. Then he narrowed the slit through which the sunlight entered, until the projected spectrum was dim indeed. Eventually his eyes adapted to the low intensity, and although color had disappeared, he was able easily to decide where in the gray band its luminous effect was greatest. He marked the place with a pencil, then opened up the slit again. His mark lay in the bluish green—well to one side of the brightest *color*. Over and over he repeated the experiment. Each test gave the same result. Blue flowers in his garden were brightest in the night because his dark-adapted eyes had higher sensitivity for this end of the spectrum. Between day and night his sensitivity shifted.

The Purkinje shift marks the transfer from vision with day-active cone cells to night-operating rods in the human retina. By day we see because of the bleaching of a pigment derived from vitamin A—iodopsin in the cone cells. At night our vision depends upon another vitamin-A derivative—the pigment rhodopsin in the rod cells. Each of these pigments absorbs light energy in a characteristic way, but the two absorptions are unlike in a manner which produces the Purkinje phenomenon.

100

Occasionally a city-dweller is dismayed to find a winding ridge raised in his grassplot, marking the runway of a mole. It is bad enough to have earthworms extend themselves at night and build piles of castings. Earthworms at least can double as fish-bait. But a mole lengthens its tunnels night and day as it searches in the upper levels of the earth for insects and worms. No matter how the land is tamped flat at supper time, the night activity raises it up again.

Often the mole seems to have arisen spontaneously. But somewhere not far away there must be a vacant lot, a neglected patch of soil. This was the staging ground for attack upon the lawn. Long after traffic ceased and the night was dark enough to be scarcely distinguishable from the subterranean blackness of the burrow, the mole emerged, perhaps crossed a paved highway. Against macadam its deep pile of dark gray fur contrasted so poorly that any prowling puss or watchful owl would have had difficulty seeing it. Indeed, for many a city person, the only evidence of shrews and moles may be those the cat brings home.

The mole's cylindrical body is ill-adapted for running over the ground's surface. Its legs seem to come from the sides instead of from below. The eyes are degenerate. No ears are visible. The tail is so brief and sticks out so stiffly that one wonders how it can have any value to the animal. But the forepaws are specialized into clawed shovels. Stout shoulders permit powerful shoving. The short neck allows the feet to reach any place where the pointed nose finds a weak spot in the soil, to thrust from there and push the earth aside. The nose itself takes no active part in loosening the soil. Instead it tests and probes at high speed, helping the mole direct its paws.

The burrower uses different techniques, according to the depth at which the tunnel is being extended. If within a few inches of the surface, space can be made by brute force. The mole turns on its side, puts the lower of the front feet against the floor at the end of its tunnel, and with the other front foot heaves against the roof. The soil gives, producing the abrupt ridge at the surface and the lengthening cavity. At greater depths, the animal may dig directly below an earlier tunnel and thrust upward from the new to block the old— transferring the cavity down a notch in this way. Or the loosened soil may be pushed by the forefeet past the body. Then the slightly webbed hindfeet take over as the mole backs up. The stubby tail guides progress in reverse, following all the curves of the passageway. Kicking and shoving, the mole drives the load of earth all the way to ground's surface. There it accumulates as a "mole hill." On a city lawn it may seem like a mountain.

Earthworms have a still different method for tunneling. At the end of the burrow, each worm uses its soft snout to push soil into its mouth. Strong suction helps take in the earth, and muscular contractions of the digestive canal transport the particles toward the other end. Any organic matter contained is food, to be broken down by ferments and absorbed into the worm's blood stream. The residue—chiefly sand—is carried in the body as a living conveyor system.

Several times a night the worm backs up to its doorway at the surface and empties out the load of earth as the familiar castings on the lawn.

The presence of many night-time visitors is not evident until morning. Then the transient's existence may have to be inferred from some calling card. A doorstep littered with sticky brown crumbs, perhaps a strange smear on the screen door—these show where a bat found temporary roost. Until the store windows along the main avenues grew dark and the house lights went out, the evening was warm enough for the flying mammal to find its fill of insects. Its first great hunger was satisfied after the day-long fast, and the bat came down to rest a while. Night after night it may choose the same site. Then, well before dawn, off it flies to feed again. Only as the eastern horizon shows streaks of day does the furry flier creep into its cranny to sleep.

The number of individual creatures that find a use for man's buildings is astonishing. In New York starlings roost in flocks around Grant's Tomb. Thousands more take shelter on the support members of the big railway bridge on upper Park Avenue. Robins incubate their eggs all night on fire escapes of the Lower East Side. Barn owls have adopted certain coal sheds along the Harlem River. Atop its offices at 1130 Fifth Avenue, the National Audubon Society has built a roof sanctuary, set out with shrubbery and feeders, for the birds to use.

Insects within a metropolis provide plenty of food for insectivorous birds. The latter in turn, find places to roost and

rear their young where buildings afford substitutes for normal habitats. The chimney swifts take their name from this
adoption of human architecture in place of hollow trees.
With fast-drying viscous saliva they cement their nests to
the inner surfaces of disused chimneys, and cling to the
brickwork from dusk to dawn. Nighthawks, which appear
over the city in the early evening, find adequate seclusion

on hot flat rooftops tarred and pebbled to exclude rain. The
eggs of these birds, and their chicks as well, are mottled in
a pattern which matches marvelously either the pebbled
roof or a spotted carpet of rocks, moss, and leaves in some
woodland.

Darkness means different things to different animals in
the city. For the diminutive hummingbird perched motion-

less on a branch, night is an enforced fast between sips of nectar. It is a time when the sugar supply in crop and blood will sink so low that to let the bird survive until morning its body temperature must drop, its nervous system grow torpid. For the tomcat, time for wooing is at hand, for caterwauling around the house where a tabby's tide is at the turn, or for seeking mice in weeds of a vacant lot.

Recently we pulled our house-trailer, lettered "Expedition for the Study of Wildlife," into a court at the New Jersey end of the George Washington Bridge. One night, before a week had passed, the wife of a New York City businessman rapped excitedly on our door. "Come quickly! There are three raccoons in a tree just back of you." And there the furry mammal family sat, watching life in a trailer colony. Behind the 'coons the skyline was bright with manmade stars: the light-studded suspension cables of the great bridge; the illuminated tower of Riverside Cathedral; and farther off, the bright summits of the Chrysler Building and Radio City. But to the mother 'coon and her half-grown youngsters, as to the United Nations, this metropolitan night was home.

EIGHT

Travelers by Night

THE periodic disappearance and reappearance of birds has led to extravagant and mistaken ideas throughout the centuries. Tall tales of swallows hibernating in mud cells like frogs in pond bottoms, then coming to life if warmed up in air, were common belief in the past. In 1703, an Englishman by the name of Morton, who signed himself as "A Person of Learning and Piety," published a pamphlet advocating the theory that birds flew to the moon for the winter. He included the perfectly correct supporting statement that in the fall they were fat and well fed, hence ready for a long journey. Two hundred and fifty thousand miles to the moon would, indeed, be a long journey—with no food or water available en route, let alone atmosphere to fly in. But the arctic terns of eastern North America travel a tenth as far each year—from the northern tip of Greenland to the antarctic continent and back. For at least 8,000 miles of this distance they are out of sight of land.

Man's planes may be grounded, but the birds take off. No doubt many of them are lost along the way. Yet the fact that substantial numbers arrive at their instinctive destinations continues to be a major marvel. Perhaps it was amazement at their daring which led Aldo Leopold to write: "One swallow does not make a summer, but one skein of geese, cleaving the murk of a March thaw, is the spring. . . . A chipmunk, emerging for a sunbath but finding a blizzard, has only to go back to bed. But a migrating goose, staking two hundred miles of black night on the chance of finding a hole in the lake, has no easy chance for retreat. His arrival carries the conviction of a prophet who has burned his bridges."

That so many birds fly at night is in itself remarkable. The bird body, as befits a flying machine, is lightly built and ill suited for colliding with branches in the dark. Moreover, most birds appear helpless without light to see by. In spite of these facts, as F. C. Lincoln has pointed out, "were we to prepare a complete list of the migratory birds of North America and note for each whether it is a day or a night traveler, it is probable that the night migrants would far outnumber those of the daylight hours. In that larger list would be found the shore birds, rails, flycatchers, orioles, most of the great family of sparrows, the wood warblers, the vireos, the wrens, the thrushes—in fact, the majority of small birds."

While it is true that the owls of night take a smaller toll of migrants than would the hawks of day, the dark hours seem paradoxically to be used for flying because vision is limited then. If the small birds migrated by day, settled in the early evening and rested a while before starting to eat, night would shut off their food supply. Seeds, fruits, insects, and little fish would be invisible until morning. Physical exhaustion without the lift of a full stomach could be fatal before daylight. On the other hand, by migrating in the dark and alighting toward dawn, the small birds can alternately rest and feed until dusk before starting onward again.

By contrast, many of the water birds which are able to find food at all hours migrate both by night and by day. Often they show no clear preference, and make a leisurely trip of the annual pilgrimage. This leaves as definite day migrants the odds and ends of the ducks and geese, the loons, cranes, gulls, pelicans, hawks, and those master aerial-ists—the swifts, swallows, and nighthawks. All of them are strong fliers, and the insectivorous ones feed as they go, diving and circling in pursuit of prey. The larger birds, and even hawks and gulls, may travel in steps, perhaps fasting for a day at a time when covering ground, then spending several days feasting at a rest stop before going on.

Time of migration appears related more to the winter home than to the number of miles flown annually or to the region where the young were raised. Birds which spend New Year's Day in the tropics are strangely punctual about coming north, seeming to go by the calendar (and length of night) rather than any vagaries of weather. They fly with such regularity that legends credit their arrival on a specific day—like the famous swallows of San Juan Capistrano in California.

Often these birds divide the flock in the fall. Adults set out separately toward the equator, as though recognizing that nesting time was over and no further need existed for staying north. Their young-of-the-year are independent (or can be) and conceal in themselves full directions for joining the parents later in the southern land.

Hardier birds, which seldom fly so far, seem to depend more upon food supplies and weather. Robins and bluebirds, Canada geese and other northern residents, move south with frost or snow. They seem ready to shift northward again as soon as winter's grip relents, and often get caught in a blizzard as a result. At each way station, robins wait until the average temperature rises above 35 degrees before progressing farther. In consequence these birds may stay as much as two months at this temperature reading, as they follow the isotherm toward their summer breeding grounds.

That so many of our birds migrate in relation to the seasons has been demonstrated abundantly during the past century and a half. Prior to that, even professional zoologists kept searching for sites in which the feathered world must hibernate. Now Ludlow Griscom regards migration as "perhaps the most distinctive phase of bird-life." Yet the seed of public misunderstanding is in this view as well. Even ornithologists, being mostly residents of the temperate zone, may fail to realize that the north-south migrations of birds each year are the familiar exception rather than the rule. Only about 15 per cent of the known kinds of birds migrate in this sense. Most of the rest—the vast majority of birds—live in the tropics and stay there.

If all birds migrated north and south each year, we could admire this talent along with their flight and feathers. But when only a minority migrate, yet demonstrate such accuracy of navigation, it is almost incredible that so special a faculty should have been developed for so few. Man prides himself on his own ability, when fog closes in around his air-borne plane, to fly "on instruments" and make safe landings at his destination. But what instruments has an air-borne migrant on a cloudy, moonless night over open ocean? For hundreds and thousands of miles the birds continue on a course which can include no detours if their slender supply of fat and glycogen is to take them to the opposite shore. They cannot be guided by recognition of the constellations, for fog does not alter their heading. The moon may be hidden. No sun can lead them through the darkness. Visual cues seem ruled out. Only two forces known to man are left, and to credit either of them seems like grasping at a straw: Can birds detect the earth's magnetic field and, if so, why are they not thrown off their courses by magnetic storms or by magnets experimentally fastened underneath their wings? Can birds utilize the "Coriolis" force resulting from the earth's rotation, even though it is so feeble?

Coriolis force deflects north-south air currents into more

easterly directions. It is possible that it could affect the fluids within the three canals of the bird's inner ear on each side, as the bird flies in any direction. It would cause a gentle flow of the fluids, and the direction of flow would alter according to the flier's heading. To make use of this information, the bird would require sensitivity within the canal system greater than any man has measured, and would need to be able to discriminate between the effects of its own head movements and those produced by the Coriolis force. Sensitivity of this kind is not impossible. It would certainly explain the otherwise inexplicable inheritance of direction sense among nestlings. How otherwise do young European storks precede the parents to their wintering grounds in South Africa? Moreover, when eggs laid by East German storks are hatched and raised in West Germany, the young fly to Africa by way of Asia Minor and the delta of the Nile (as do their parents), instead of going with the West German storks by way of Spain and Gibraltar.

To gain the greatest effect from the Coriolis force, a flying bird would need to turn its head from side to side and compare the fluid movements within its canals. Any turning of the head would upset the air flow over the feathers. This would increase pressure on the eardrum of one side, decrease it on the other, and no doubt make it difficult for the bird to estimate events in the inner ear.

As recently as 1951, William J. Beecher discovered an apparent answer to this problem. In birds that migrate mainly at night, there is a special membranous sac lining the bony wall of the auditory canal leading from the outside world to the eardrum. Contraction of a muscle associated with the eardrum dams a vein and fills the sac with blood, thereby enlarging it and blocking the auditory canal. The assumption is that whenever night-flying migrants turn their heads in flight to use their inner-ear canals as gyrocompasses, they inflate the sacs and keep the unequal air pressure from disturbing their eardrums. Geese, swans, and the diurnal ducks —which use visual cues in migration—lack this inflatable sac. Only the ruddy duck has it, and this bird habitually migrates at night. The fact that birds which, because of nocturnal migrating habits, are most in need of navigational aid possess the inflatable sac is circumstantial evidence favoring the Coriolis-force theory of direction-finding.

Man has corresponding canals in each inner ear, but his natural speed over the ground is too slow for the Coriolis force to help guide him. Perhaps the minimum is just below the average flight speed of small birds—twenty to twenty-five miles per hour. Bats, however, are flying mammals with the same inner-ear equipment. Many of them migrate. All find their way about in the dark with an ability often described as uncanny. No inflatable plug for the outer ear is found in bats, but they do have a series of valve-like cartilages at the opening of the auditory canal. These might function to close off air-pressure changes from the eardrum during the brief head-turning movements required if the bat is to use Coriolis-force effects in the inner ears as a compass. It is clear that bats must use their ears to hear their own echoed ultrasonic calls in ranging on obstacles and food. Accordingly, it is suggested that they employ their ear valves only momentarily in homing or migrating, just as is possible among the night-migrating birds.

That flying creatures which find their way through the dark so well have a means for closing off the outer ear suggests that there might be a correlation elsewhere in the animal kingdom between migrating habits and a similar ear mechanism. On land the other mammals able to close their ears are the armadillo, the hedgehog, and the pangolin—all of which burrow and presumably need to keep the dirt out. In water, the seals and whales have pencil-sized auditory canals which they can close. This ability has always been assumed to be an adaptation to diving, but it could be helpful in direction-finding as well. Turtles and fishes, many of which exhibit homing and migration, have no outer ear to block off.

Whatever the means permitting accurate navigation in the night, "by the power of their wings, migratory birds have so covered the earth that there is hardly a spot they do not regularly visit." Formerly it was believed that, to avoid flying into obstacles, they rose to elevations greater than 15,000 feet, even over level land or water. Now it is realized that birds will attain high altitudes—even to 20,000 feet or better —in crossing mountain ranges, but immediately they descend again to their normal traveling altitude. In general, they fly below 3,000 feet. Many skim along just a few feet over the waves, apparently in an effort to avoid adverse winds in the upper air. Occasionally a sudden storm strikes these low fliers and drives them into the water, where they drown. On land similar low-altitude flying can introduce difficulties. Repeatedly the Lapland longspurs of the Middle West run into snowstorms which drag them down in the darkness to die of exposure and exhaustion on the open prairies.

Some estimate of the number of low-flying migrants may be formed from the numbers that are killed from collision with lighthouses, tall buildings, radio towers, power lines, and telegraph wires. In many instances it is evident that the birds simply failed to see the obstruction. In others, the man-made obstacle serves as a distraction. Apparently it induces the flier to transfer its navigation from the built-in gyro-compass (however it operates) to visual cues. In clear weather, these fatalities at lighted structures are infrequent. But in fog or storm, the numbers mount rapidly.

For some reason a fixed white stationary light is more disastrous to the migrants than is a flashing beam or a red lamp. The Washington Monument (555 feet high) accounted for many deaths until lighting around it became sufficient for the migrants to detect it. Later, when special floodlighting was added in 1931, the shaft became so brilliant as to confuse birds in a fog or a storm, and deaths mounted again. Similarly, the torch of the Statue of Liberty (305 feet above the ground) destroyed as many as seven hundred birds in a month until its intensity was reduced.

To a considerable degree, deaths at beacons and tall illuminated buildings seem caused by overexertion of the bewildered migrant, which tries to fly onward into the obstruction and has no place to rest while regaining orientation. Wire screens in front of lighthouse glass panels, and various kinds of perches and shelves on which the fliers can settle temporarily, have done much to reduce the casualties.

Various methods have been used to study migrants in the night. Around the turn of the century, William Beebe spent a night atop the Statue of Liberty, trying to recognize the birds as they passed through the lighted air. More recently, Edwin Way Teale has attempted a census from the roof of the Empire State Building (1,472 feet high), the tallest of

the six structures in New York which extend skyward beyond the 750-foot mark. But the sampling is meager. So is
the occasional count of birds that settle during the dawn
hours on the rigging of ships at sea, although the British
Ornithologists' Club has conscientiously tabulated every
scrap of information available.

When World War II was at its height in Europe, night-
migrating birds disturbed Britain time after time. One of the
earliest episodes occurred in November of 1941. Along the
east coast of England north of London, all of the sirens and
invasion-alarm systems went into action because moving
spots appeared on the new radar screens. But instead of
planes or ships, the gun crews and aircraft spotters heard the
honking of geese flying toward feeding grounds at the mouth
of the Humber River. When higher powered radar equipment was installed in 1943, the difficulty grew greater. Even
small birds and those high up were seen as pips on the
screen. It became necessary to educate radar operators in
distinguishing bird from plane by suspending dead gulls
from captive balloons, and swinging them back and forth!
Now, whenever military cooperation allows the luxury, stu-
dents of migration try to use radar tracking to learn altitudes,
speed, and course for each kind of bird. One goose was followed for more than an hour and a half, streaking along at
a steady thirty-five miles per hour.

The moon is a great help in observing bird movements at
night. No doubt its light assists the fliers too, for the number
of shore birds winging along the coast rises perceptibly

when the moon is shining. A few seem to wait to take advantage of the nocturnal light.

About the time that the descendants of the Pilgrim Fathers were framing a Declaration of Independence, an Italian naturalist (Giovanni A. Scopoli) recorded that the woodcock traveled northward through his area of Yugoslavia during the full moon in March. It returned southbound at the corresponding phase in October. The northbound birds continued on toward Scandinavia and the British Isles, still by moonlight. Gilbert White, just south of London, thought it "probable that woodcocks in moonshiny nights cross the German Ocean from Scandinavia." He asked his correspondents to help get information: "At present I do not know anybody near the sea-side that will take the trouble to remark at what time of the moon woodcocks first come."

Since 1946, under the careful guidance of George H. Lowery, Jr., and Robert J. Newman of Louisiana State University, the study of night migrants under the moon has taken a new and more precise turn. Encouraged by these two ornithologists, upwards of two hundred observers in Canada, in the various states of the U.S.A. and in Mexico, have sat hour after hour with field glasses and telescopes fixed on the moon itself. They tally birds, bats, and even large moths as these fly between the satellite and their instruments.

Each observer examines a piece of sky consisting of an inverted cone extending slenderly from telescope to moon— the "observation cone." From hour to hour, as the moon

rises and sets, the amount of atmosphere within the observation cone changes rapidly. When the moon is high, the
narrow cone includes relatively little air of importance to
birds—below their usual flight ceiling. But when the moon
is low, the cone slants through a tremendous observation
space before it projects beyond the curved atmosphere to a
height from the ground of a mile or two. Hence two birds
crossing the moon's disc per hour when the moon is high rep-
resent a far greater number migrating than two birds seen
against the moon shortly after it has risen.

From a record of the date and hour, and the direction
taken by each bird silhouetted against the moon, an expert
can compute the compass heading of the migrant. When this
information is plotted on weather maps, new facts on how
and when birds travel emerge for study. The task of process-
ing the observations is tremendous. But it is safe to assume
that the vast majority of birds in the upper air are there for
one purpose only—to migrate. This provides at night, as seldom during daylight hours, a spatial separation between
birds that are migrating and those that are not.

Of course, more questions are raised than are answered by
studies of birds against the moon. Yet each question delves
more deeply into the migratory instinct and represents progress in our attempt to understand it. The number of birds
that fly all night seems small. More of them rest in the early
evening, then spiral upward and strike out in the proper
direction, only to subside after a few hours. The maximum
number seems to be active around midnight.

At night each bird appears to be more on its own. Flocks of migrants are far less frequent than during the day. Instead the nocturnal fliers are dispersed rather uniformly. Moreover, they show a remarkable correlation with air currents in their direction of flight, suggesting that "most night migrants may travel by a system of pressure-pattern flying." Occasionally, on a particular night in spring, most of the birds have been observed flying *southward*—obviously confused enough—although by an unknown factor—to go the wrong way!

One of the delightful aspects in this scientific study of nocturnal migration is that, when no birds happen to be passing, the moon is still there to admire. Even the 48-page instruction manual issued to observers by the Louisiana State University finds place to tuck in a few pages of information about the satellite. If a few clouds drift across the night sky, the earth's companion becomes the poet's "ghostly galleon." No wonder William Beebe thought of a current when he wrote in 1906: "As a projecting pebble in midstream blurs the transparent water with a myriad bubbles, so the narrow path of moon-rays, which our glass reveals, cuts a swath of visibility straight through the host of birds to our eager eyes. . . . Now and then we recognize the flight of some particular species—the swinging loop of a woodpecker or goldfinch, or the flutter of a sandpiper. . . . Migration is at its height, the chirps and twitters which come from the surrounding darkness are tantalizing hints telling of the passing legions. Thousands and thousands of birds are . . . pouring northward in a swift, invisible, aerial stream."

To learn how far the feathered fliers go we rely on the recovery of aluminum bracelets fitted to a bird's leg by one person and returned by another. Most of these bands bear a serial number and the words "Write Fish and Wildlife Service, Washington, D.C., U.S.A." Those that return as directed are entered on punch cards in the tremendous file at the research laboratory in Laurel, Maryland. Each banded bird has its own card, bearing information on species and sex, where banded, when, and by whom. Each time it is re-captured, additional entries are made on the card. Although only a small percentage of the birds tagged in this way each year are ever recovered, the information obtained from the few is worth while.

Sometimes the migration direction is surprising: a robin banded in March near Philadelphia, caught the following August in Newfoundland; a purple finch tagged in New Hampshire in August, picked up 1,500 miles away in Texas the next January, a snow bunting given a number in Michigan, picked up in Greenland two months later.

Both the person who attaches a band and the one who returns it receive from the custodians of the file cards a history of the individual flier—a unique form of "thank you" for their cooperation. In this way a native hunter in British Honduras learned that the blue heron he shot had been tagged in Wisconsin. The bander of a barn swallow in Saskatchewan was advised that bird number so-and-so had been recovered in Bolivia. From Maine a catbird flew to Honduras and was caught. A white-crowned sparrow from Maine went to Georgia. There it could have met banded bluebirds from Cape Cod and nighthawks from North Dakota. All these are known from the bracelets.

The first bird banding in America involved phoebes—flycatchers which migrate by night. In 1803, John J. Audubon fastened loose circlets of silver wire around an ankle of each fledgeling in a nest he had under observation, and then watched for them to return the following year to the same creek in Pennsylvania. Two out of five did—an exceptionally high rate of return.

In Europe, a Danish ornithologist, H. C. C. Mortensen, began about 1899 to place numbered bands on storks and several other kinds of birds. Leon J. Cole brought the method to America in 1901, and the following year Paul Bartsch of the Smithsonian Institution began using tags marked "Return to Smithsonian." By 1904, a whole series of handmade bands were being applied in Canada by P. A. Taverner and his correspondents.

It seems strange that, a century after Audubon's experiment, bird banding was organized on an international scale all within a five-year period. So important did the work become that in 1920 it was taken over in America by the U.S. Biological Survey, and administered as a federal propect under the Migratory Bird Treaty with Canada and Mexico. At present, some 300,000 birds annually are tagged by around 2,100 banding stations. Approximately 20,000 of these bands are seen again each year, either on trapped live birds or on dead ones.

Night-feeding insectivorous birds, such as nighthawk and whippoorwill, migrate by day. Day-feeding insectivorous birds, such as phoebes and flycatchers, migrate at night. Bats both feed and migrate at night, and take the trip by steps that permit them to eat well along the way. This may be due partly to the fewness of their enemies. As they travel through the darkness, bats are so much safer than birds. In fact, no other nocturnal aviator of similar size can approach their record.

To learn more about migratory and other habits in bats, a study has begun in recent years, using numbered aluminum clips fastened rather loosely to their wings. Within minutes after a bat is born, a tag of this type can be attached around a bone corresponding to man's forearm. Its presence does not interfere with growth, nursing, or flight. With care, every bat in a bat roost can be captured for attachment of a tag or inspection of the number given it before. As a result, even though so few years have gone into their observation, a great deal has been learned about their ways.

A measure of bat survival is obtained by checking a nesting colony at annual intervals to learn which banded individuals have returned. About 80 per cent of the adults present on one inspection trip will be there again a year later. The average age of adult bats in a colony of this kind is five years. Birds of comparable size have a much smaller chance of survival, and their average age is not much over one year.

Mice of similar weight and nocturnal habits are even more regularly decimated by predators. A year-old meadow mouse in the wild is something of a patriarch! But corresponding to each way of life is a rate of reproduction: one baby per bat mother per year; two four-egg clutches for the small bird; perhaps thirteen litters averaging six young apiece for a meadow mouse. Reproduction must match the

regular losses or an animal kind will disappear from existence. Putting numbered tags on bats and birds is more worth while than banding short-lived animals such as mice.

Part of the success of bats in the race for survival arises from their ability to feed efficiently, whether in their northern summer homes, their southern wintering grounds, or on the way between the two. The little brown bat *Myotis*, emerging hungry at dusk, has been recorded as collecting a fifth of its own weight in insects within two hours. Pipistrelles of the eastern states are smaller yet even more efficient—catching a quarter of their body weight in a half hour of furious feeding. One at a time they pursue gnats of 3-mm wingspread and moths of 20-mm. They tear the wings from each, or chew their prey whole and swallow it. An hourly catch must number somewhere between 5,000 gnats and 66 moths, since either of these totals would include the right weight of insect prey. The detection and pursuit of so many individual victims by ultrasonic ranging within a 60-minute period gives some explanation for the seemingly erratic flight of feeding bats. They may be catching gnats faster than one a second.

That bats can drink from a pool or stream while flying above it surprises the uninitiated. The tropical bat *Noctilio* has specialized hind feet and uses these to capture small fish from ponds and rivers, wherever the minnows are numerous near the surface. *Noctilio*'s calls are more complex than most, but the evidence indicates that they do not echo-locate individual victims. They may find schools of fish through use of their remarkable voices and hearing.

Bats have a special feast whenever their paths meet a migrating swarm of moths. By morning the ground may be littered with discarded wings, as though they were petals fallen from a flowering tree.

Nor can anyone explain the moths' migration. Most famous of them is the "cotton-worm moth," *Alabama argillacea*. In the spring this insect appears from some unknown source in Central America, and breeds for several disastrous generations on the cotton crops of the southern United States.

Then, instead of returning southward, thousands or even millions of the adult insects set out on another northward course. With help from the wind they may reach Canada, arriving in such enormous numbers as to slow traffic. They come to lighted store fronts and cover the windows. None of them survive. No progeny of theirs fly in the opposite direction. Depending on breezes which help them onward, they reach different parts of the country each year. How the supply of cotton-worm moths is replenished is a mystery, but somewhere in the American tropics they must have a natural home.

Both the annual round trips of birds and bats and the one-way flight of the insects are given the name migration. It is clear that the term is used loosely. Yet for each of these mass movements by air, corresponding events on the ground are known. Accurately matching the butterflies and moths which wing their way out to sea by the millions, never to return, are the frequent eruptions of lemmings in northern Europe. These small, mouse-like denizens of higher land in the arctic and subarctic regions reproduce far faster than their food supply—lichens and mosses. By late winter or spring the majority must move or starve. They migrate by the thousands, chiefly by night, driving themselves down the valleys, through the sedges, past the spruces, in one concerted, frantic rush. A lake, a pond, a slow-flowing stream, provides no barrier. They swim across. The larger fish devour them until stomachs will hold no more. Owls, foxes, wolves, lynxes, wolverines, and bears eat practically nothing but lemmings while the hysteria is on. Even reindeer (caribou) change to a meat diet during the migration. If a fast river or stormy lake or even the ocean bars the way, these rodents strike out to cross it—swimming until they are exhausted and drown. None come back. The population in the highlands starts again, almost from scratch, parented by the few who remained behind. For them the sparse food supply is adequate. In a few years (or even one good season if, for some reason, the predators relent), the lemmings are so numerous again that migration leads the way to mass suicide.

On land a two-way migration cannot be expected to cover as much territory as in the air. Usually it is recognized in seasonal movements such as the elk make at night. As the mating season ends in the fall, the bulls with their magnificent antlers and their little harems of cow elk move down the mountain slopes through the forested land. By the time snow arrives the herds are converging on each valley, where sedges and grasses can be pawed for and the snow will not grow so deep. All winter they feed in the bottom land. Antlers drop and the buds of new ones appear. The snow turns to streams. Bushes grow misty with fresh leaves. Night after night the elk move up the valleys, keeping time with spring, enjoying the fresh foliage. The green twigs lead them back to the mountain fastnesses for summer days.

How far the concept of migration can be extended is still unsettled. So many examples seem to require expert navigation of an unproven type. A mother tern arises in the night, flies to the water, and soon returns from sea to land with a crop full of fish to disgorge for her hungry young—all in the dark. No one knows how she finds her way on the return trip, for other nests may be within a foot or two. Some of them contain equally hungry young, waiting for a parent out at sea.

A baby puffin, stuffed with food and then deserted by its parents, grows on its fat store for a week, alone in its rock cranny or burrow. Then, in complete darkness, when gulls and other enemies are asleep, the flightless young bird waddles and tumbles toward the ocean from its island ledge. Morning finds it swimming and diving, ready to vanish below the surface whenever a gull swoops low. It must learn to catch fish and to fly while out of sight of others of its kind—a solitary chick braving the waves.

Next year, if it is still alive, the puffin will return on wings, fly to the same rock ledge and, with adolescent curiosity, inspect another generation repeating the same pattern. No one knows how the puffin finds its way back. As it migrates to the water in darkness, it is out of its shaded burrow for the first time. Surely it cannot see enough as it steps along so deliberately, ocean-bound, to identify this particular ledge from all others when next year it flies back. When its wings are strong enough to lift it from the waves for an aerial inspection of its birthplace, the young puffin is miles away, already working southward to warmer regions in which it will spend the winter.

The arrival of migrating birds was a miracle as long ago as

the writing of the sixteenth chapter of Exodus: "And the Lord spake unto Moses, saying, I have heard the murmurings of the children of Israel: speak unto them, saying, At even ye shall eat flesh. . . . And it came to pass, that at even the quails came up, and covered the camp."

NINE

Dark Waterways

Until 1946, California had a flourishing fisheries industry geared to the phases of the moon. All day, and all night whenever the moon was above the horizon, its boats were tied idly at the docks; its canneries were closed down. But in spite of this seeming indolence, the industry processed a quarter of the total tonnage of fish caught along American shores, and directly supported some 25,000 people. Now it is in decline, for the one fish on which it was based has suddenly and inexplicably decreased in abundance.

Californians call the fish "sardines." In Oregon and Washington they go by the name of "pilchard." All are young herring. For some curious reason, their habits off the California coast make them most vulnerable to fishermen in the dead of night, by the dark of the moon. Only then can a sharp-eyed lookout, cruising back and forth through the

fishing grounds, detect in the black water the faint pond-sized areas of light which tell where sardines are feeding near the surface. From the dimensions of the "pool" they can tell whether the school of fish is large enough to be worth wrapping up in a net.

If the luminous area is a big one, two men start out for it in a skiff, using no lights and making no sound or vibration that they can avoid. Behind them they pay out one end of a net. Gradually they work around the school of fish until the circle of cork floats is complete. Then, cautiously they draw the lines which purse the seine into a cup-shaped web—and the fish are theirs. Floodlights can be turned on, the net pulled slowly into the mother ship, and the sardines brailed into the hold. A hundred tons is regarded as a good catch. As much as four hundred tons from a single seineful has been reported.

Sardines themselves are not luminous. The dim light in the dark water arises from single-celled forms of life drifting near the surface, stirred to luminescence by the swirling movements of the feeding fish. The display has the same origin as was described by Charles Darwin when the *Beagle* "drove before her bows two billows of liquid phosphorous, and in her wake she was followed by a milky train. As far as the eye reached, the crest of every wave was bright."

For the most part, the sardines are not eating these particular microscopic organisms. Instead, they are straining from the water great numbers of small crustaceans—diminutive relatives of the "water fleas" in ponds—which browse, in turn, upon microscopic green plants, chiefly unicellular algae. Whether the fish are at the surface by day as well as by night is unknown. Their presence in upper waters would depend not only upon the ways of sardines themselves but also upon the habits of their primary food, the small crustaceans.

Intense study is being given to the decrepit sardine fishery in an attempt to bring it back. New information on pertinent subjects includes a better understanding of the "pastures of the sea" in which sardines swim.

Often the first contribution of the scientist is to relate vague observations made over a long time. For example, sailors have known for years that the surface water changes color mile after mile. Those men who have remained stationary for a month or so—as on a lightship anchored near a reef—realize that the same area of ocean alters from blue to green and back again, time after time as the weeks go by. This slow modification in color is due chiefly to a "blooming" as microscopic plants reproduce rapidly. Their incredible numbers give a tint to the surface—the color of chlorophyll.

Each area of algal bloom affords a feasting ground for small crustaceans. To it they swim from all directions. Within a few days the well-fed little animals are reproducing at top speed. Soon their numbers are so great that they threaten the continued existence of the algae. Even if fish discover the crustaceans and reduce their net rate of increase, a situation is reached in which the green food supply diminishes. The sea locally loses both its visible green color and its attraction for crustaceans. To eat they must move on, into greener pastures.

If a time-lapse movie record could be made of a square mile of sea surface, the slow changes in color could be pictured with ease. As each patch turned green, paying in food the many crustaceans migrating in that direction, it would be possible to point to blue regions from which the animal life had almost disappeared. Algae there have new opportunity to reproduce relatively unmolested, and soon a new patch of bloom appears. The dappling of blue and green pulsates with a regular rhythm, though with no design or pattern.

Most crustaceans avoid daylight. Even before dawn, these

diminutive relatives of the lobster have already started to kick themselves down through the dark water away from the surface and the algae there. As sunset fades and the sea grows black again, they climb to feed through another night. Presumably the sardines disperse too when their food supply no longer is concentrated at the surface.

Although the three-dimensional character of the crustaceans' movements is now better appreciated, the complex factors that govern their food supply—the algae—include many unknowns. The greatest concentration of these plants is in regions where water currents bring dissolved minerals from the bottom toward the surface, as upwellings of fertilizer to the oceanic pasture. The currents, in turn, depend for their velocity and direction upon prevailing winds (often far away) and upon the contours of the continents.

Variations in weather not only affect the winds, but also may suddenly alter the rainfall on the land. This latter modifies the coastal currents through changes in the amount of fresh water pushing outward from each major river's mouth. The mixing of fresh water and salty ocean affect the sea's salinity along the coast. Temperature can vary too. And each modification away from what the microscopic plants are used to can so depress their reproductive rate that the pyramid of animal numbers depending on the algae crumbles without obvious cause.

The changeability of conditions in the ocean tends to conceal one central constancy: it is at night that most animal life is active. The worms, crabs, eels, flounders, and larval stages of bigger fish all emerge from hiding to feast on small crustaceans. Swarms of jellyfish pulse through the black water, trailing tentacles to which living food adheres. Snapping shrimp reach repeatedly for prey, and the sizzling sound of their feeding may be loud enough to be audible to man. On the blackest nights some South Sea fishermen can guide their boats by this "natural bell buoy, a warning of reefs and shallows for all who can hear and comprehend." Both their need of this aid to navigation and the sound itself vanishes in the dawn, when the host of swimming creatures disperse.

Through all this flux of life within the sea, night sees many a migration ending with the birth of new individuals hopefully starting out. The salmon and the eel, the smelt and the lamprey, the seal and the whale, each swims through the dark waterways toward a meeting place with others of its kind. They match their lives to the year, to the moon-made tides, and to the shadows which, from sunset to dawn, spread safety upon the waters.

Perhaps the most spectacular of these night swimmers is a segmented worm, the palolo, which grows to a length of a foot or so in coral-reef crannies of the South Seas. At the third quarter of the moon in October comes the "little rising," and twenty-eight days later the "great rising"—nights on which enormous numbers of these creatures swim at the surface in a mating dance concealed by darkness. Native islanders, who relish the egg-laden female palolos as food, not only watch for their appearance but even schedule tribal festivities to match the date. Then, before midnight, the men paddle out toward the reefs and watch by torchlight to dip up each worm that swirls within reach.

In the 1890's, an expedition headed by Alexander Agassiz of Harvard took advantage of its presence in the Fiji Islands to study the palolo. Even the solemn scientific report pub-

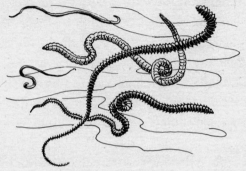

lished in the 1897 *Bulletin of the Museum of Comparative Zoölogy* cannot conceal the excitement. Canoe after canoe returned with a load of wriggling worms. Islanders were so eager to reach the delicacy that they ate them "quite undressed." The scientists waited for cooked worms, which were served hot, wrapped in leaves of the breadfruit tree. The dish had an appearance suggesting spinach; it smelled and tasted "not unlike fresh fish's roe."

Closer examination of the live worms disclosed a fact which had escaped the attention of the Fijians. Each body was headless. No matter how carefully the creatures were caught, the forward end always was missing.

The headless bodies behaved as though each were a complete individual. They swam in circles and spiral paths visible in the torchlight. Occasionally an egg-laden female would be surrounded by a group of smaller males. If they touched her in passing, a cloud of mingled eggs and sperm cells would burst out into the water, and soon sink toward the bottom as developing embryos starting off a new generation of palolos. It seemed incredible that so complex a behavior should be carried on without benefit of the main parts of the nervous system. Yet only the head end contains the worm's counterpart of a brain.

Many years later a partial answer to this nocturnal puzzle was found by fresh study of the coral reefs. It turned out that the whole worm becomes mature in season by concentrating either eggs or sperms in the hinder half of its body. This posterior portion develops eyespots along the mid line below each segment. When the phase of the moon is right in October or November, the two halves of the animal part company in the early evening. The headless part swims to the surface. The rest of the worm remains as a parent in the coral crannies and grows a new posterior portion in time for a repeat performance the following year.

In its third quarter, the moon has barely risen at the time the mating dance is over. Clearly the worms do not wait for it as a signal to separate, in the reef rocks far below the surface. Perhaps, the scientists thought, the tides were responsible. To test the theory, they imprisoned coral chunks and worms together in floating cages which rose and fell with the water movements—never getting deeper or shallower no matter how the moon distorted the oceans. These worms swarmed when their fellows in the reefs came out.

Perhaps the moon's light was responsible. At sunset the floating cages were roofed with opaque covers, and the experiment was started more than a month before the "great rising." At dawn each day the shades were removed again. None of the covered worms responded to the mating urge. One conclusion was inescapable: somehow the worms detected the moonlight and its cyclic changes. On nights prior to the swarming, the moon showed itself more and more briefly, rising later and with less of its disc bright. This regular decrease in nocturnal illumination must set an internal clock, geared to go off on the proper night. After sunset on this special date the mating alarm stimulates the worms to swarm. Neap tide and rainy season merely happen to match.

Palolo worms migrate vertically only a relatively short distance through the night. Other swimmers travel horizontally for thousands of miles. Of these the eel is justly famous. Even in landlocked ponds far from the sea, females eight years old and more reach maturity, their ovaries loaded with as many as a hundred thousand minute eggs. Each female's body is sleek and fat, seemingly in the prime of life. Suddenly these eels cease feeding. Their backs grow more intensely black. Sides and bellies take on a silvery sheen. Eyes enlarge, and the front pair of fins turn blackish, becoming at the same time more pointed. Then, in an autumn night, these almost scaleless fish writhe up on the shore and set out, when the fields are wet with dew, for the nearest stream. They stand exposure to air for a second night if the first does not get them to their watery destination. Few fail.

Once in a creek, the eels rest by day and travel downstream by nightly stages. Eventually they reach salt water and there meet a congregation of male eels, each somewhat shorter—three feet instead of as much as five in length—many of them silvery white like the migrating females. The better part of a week is spent in becoming acclimated to the salinity of the open ocean, before the silvery ones swim into the outer depths and aim toward the Sargasso Sea, south of Bermuda. Eels from Europe (but not the Mediterranean), from North Africa and West Africa, from the Atlantic coast of North America, all converge on this one region—the center of the great North Atlantic eddy.

In depths of the Sargasso from 650 to 1,800 feet below the surface, the eels mate and lay. No one knows whether the parents continue to live there—resuming an interest in food—or die and disintegrate. None are seen again. The migration pattern itself was worked out only in 1925, when an outstanding Danish scientist, Johannes Schmidt, followed by boat the path taken by young eels on their way from the Sargasso to the rivers from which their parents came. He did not find the eggs. That achievement is credited to one of the research people, Marie Poland Fish, aboard the *Arcturus* expedition to the Sargasso Sea in the following year. Three strange fish eggs attached to the shell of a crab dredged up from the bottom hatched into young eels in the laboratory aboard ship.

Newborn eels are buoyant enough so that they drift upward to the surface, there to feed on microscopic algae. The young eels are so unlike the parents in shape and behavior that a special name was given to them—leptocephali. The body is laterally compressed, thin as a leaf, and so transparent that the vertebrae of the backbone can be counted in the living animal. For many years leptocephali were known but their relationship to eels was never guessed. Now it is evident that even at this early stage, European and African eels can be distinguished from the American ones, since the latter have a few less vertebrae.

After about a year of drifting in the upper layers of the Sargasso Sea, the leptocephali of all the eels have grown more vigorous, although their body form is much the same. Gradually they migrate northwestward until they reach the Gulf Stream, which in turn sweeps them northeast along the Atlantic coast of America.

The leptocephali of North American eels leave the Gulf Stream one after another, to swim west and reach the coastal rivers. In the brackish water of the mouth each transforms in body form to more eel-like proportions, to become an "elver." Then the elvers start up the stream, resting by day and traveling at night—just as their parents did on the way down. By this time each is two or three inches long and the season is spring. Males are not so persistent as females. The latter work their way into the headwaters. Males remain in the lower parts of each river, usually where there is still some salinity.

European leptocephali remain with the Gulf Stream for another two years or so, and are carried across the Atlantic to their homelands. Why they are to mature into elvers ("glass eels") later than the American leptocephali, and for this reason can wait through the longer trip, is still a mystery. So is the route taken by the African eels. None are known to make a mistake. In Europe, where many of the rivers come from high in mountain areas, eels sometimes reach 8,000 feet elevation before they settle down to feed as scavengers in the marshy streams and ponds. In cold weather, if the pond freezes over, eels can hibernate—buried in the mud—and emerge when the water warms up the following spring.

In America, silver eels migrating toward the sea at night are trapped by the million. About 650 tons of them are sold for approximately $25,000 each year. Many are held in cages from the time of their autumn migration until just before

Christmas, to appeal to markets that favor eel meat as a holiday dish. Since these are the eels that automatically have stopped eating—depending on their food reserves to carry them all the way to the Sargasso Sea—they need not be fed in live storage.

Accompanying the elvers in their ascent of the streams on spring nights—and fighting equally hard against the strong current—are larger fish of the same cylindrical body form. Lamprey "eels" from the sea move into fresh water to lay their eggs. They are jawless creatures with a sucking mouth full of rasping teeth. Even the piston-like tongue is so armed. Along each side of the body runs a row of portholes—the openings of pouch-like gills which inhale and exhale the water whenever the circular mouth is clamped to some support.

Night after night the lampreys move up toward the headwaters. Days are spent inconspicuously clinging to a stone or wharf piling. Eventually the stream narrows, and in the darkness the lampreys change their behavior. Females begin to rest for short intervals. Males are more restless. They attach their sucker mouths to one solid object after another. Occasionally they find a second lamprey and take hold of it. If the lamprey to which a male affixes himself is another male, the latter lets go of the support and the two drift downstream, soon to separate. Up the current they scull themselves, to try their luck once more. By contrast, a female remains attached when a male places his sucking mouth on her body. This difference seems to be the clue allowing a

141

pair to identify one another. Their eyes are too degenerate to help—even if there were light in the dark water.

After a time, the two lampreys shift position, but without losing contact with one another. Touch is their guide and they stay close together. Moving toward the side of the stream, they reach a position where the current is slow, perhaps in some shallow area. There the male (and sometimes also his mate) commences to pick up stones, using his mouth to lift and carry each to one side. When a clean sandy bottom has been exposed, the female moves over and deposits her eggs—sometimes over 200,000 of them in a single area. The male fertilizes them in batches. Later both lampreys move slightly upstream from the fertilized eggs and once more begin shifting stones. Sand disturbed by the current and by the eels drifts down over the eggs and hides them from enemy eyes.

Parent sea lampreys usually die without returning to the ocean. The young, called "ammocetes," feed in the muddy marshes on microscopic plants and animals for four or five years before transforming into fish parasites equipped for rasping a hole in their victim and drinking its blood. Since streams have few fish numerous and large enough to feed mature lampreys, the young parasites usually drift downstream night after night to reach the ocean, and there prey on whatever they can catch. Sea lampreys are numerous along the Atlantic coast of North America as far as Florida, of northern Europe, and northwestern Africa. Those that have managed to enter Lake Champlain and the Great Lakes never return to salt water, and do great damage to the fresh-water fisheries.

Lampreys are most conspicuous on a spring night, when the three-foot adults are entering rivers from the ocean. Like so many animated blackish hoses, they swim and clamber over dams and around rapids, desperate in their eagerness to reach a place to mate.

Far smaller animals take advantage of the wetness of spring nights to migrate from stream to stream, to pond, to marsh. Crayfish emerge from the water by the dozens. They step along on springy legs, their great feelers flicking far in front, extended in search of danger. If dawn finds them still in an open field, they hurriedly dig a vertical burrow into the soil. Around the opening they throw up excavated mud into a "chimney" which helps both to hide the crustacean and to keep the sun from reaching the bottom of its temporary resting place.

Along the southern Mississippi valley, where rice fields and corn patches retain water a few inches below the surface all through the summer, crayfish may make a more permanent home in an excavated cavern with a constant film of moisture on the floor. There they can feed on roots which grow through the roof—to the serious detriment of the crops. There is no easy way to reach them through gumbo soils. Even raccoons have difficulty catching the crustaceans through their narrow doorways. Yet each night the crayfish can emerge, to wander freely and feed at will upon any greenery within reach.

Occasionally a motorist sees in his headlight beams a few dozens of these pale crayfish crossing the blacktop through a marshy spot. More usually, no one notes the migration of these aquatic creatures in the dead of night. A more common discovery along the same type of narrow roadway is an army of frogs or toads hopping from one side to the other, on their way to the annual spring meeting in a pond. The

amphibians may bump into one another, yet none show any recognition, like of like, or male of female. For the moment the urge to travel toward the pond is drive enough. Only when they have reached the water, and each is in a place so wet that fertilized eggs can hatch into tadpoles of midnight black, will they raise their voices or hurry toward a mate.

A far rarer discovery is the sudden migration of six- to seven-inch spotted salamanders through a March or April rain at dusk. All of them scramble along with their black bodies glistening and bellies flat against the ground. Anywhere in the Mississippi drainage area or eastward to the Atlantic seaboard, these large, tailed salamanders show an uncanny ability to choose the same night for moving. Out from their winter hiding places below the frost line in the woods they emerge. Perhaps because the males are of lesser weight, they reach the water before the females do. The pond may be still rimmed with ice, but the ardor of these animals is not lessened. Busily they patrol the edge, as though keeping continuous watch for their tardy ladies.

One at a time the female spotted salamanders reach the pond and drop into the water. Before each female as many as fifty males undulate in an aquacade, approaching, sensing her nearness, yet seldom disturbing her with a touch. Apparently their presence brings her excitement to a peak that they can detect. Suddenly every male dives to the bottom, straddles a leaf edge or twig or stone, and deposits a small pyramid of jelly topped with a white cap of sperm suspension. The males stand aside. Now it is the female's turn. Delicately she descends to the garden of sperm caps on jelly mounds and, with the sensitive lips of her reproductive opening, she picks up one or more. The rest go to waste.

Soon the salamander mother begins to liberate small masses of minute eggs surrounded by a mucus-like secretion. The material quickly absorbs water, until each egg clump swells into a fist-sized mass. Enclosed and protected by the jelly are perhaps a hundred embryos.

With the next night rain, all of the spotted salamanders leave the pond and return to the wood. There they can spend another year hunting through the moist soil for worms and insects. Again there is an opportunity to find them in migration, although this time the real show is over. The discovery is only a parade. Its meaning lives in the pond.

TEN

Sea-old Night

THE sea hides the most everlasting night of all. When the cooling earth first reached a temperature at which liquid water could exist, the low places filled as the primeval oceans. Perpetual night was cupped in their depths. To modern man, sailing over the surface, it seems incongruous that a liquid so transparent in a tumbler or bucket should be so opaque as to conceal its bottom. Yet despite the clarity of ocean water, sunlight does not penetrate far.

Even the clearest sea water is more or less turbid with suspended opaque particles and floating organisms. It is far different from a pure saline solution, and the depth to which daylight penetrates at noon varies not only with latitude but also with the degree of turbidity. The waters of the Sargasso Sea in the Atlantic Ocean near Bermuda, and of the Mediterranean Sea, are the clearest ones known. In the Sargasso, all but one per cent of surface light has been absorbed at a depth of 495 feet (82.5 fathoms—149 meters). A hundred and six feet have this same effect in the Gulf of Maine, whereas the finely divided silt and many small living creatures in the harbor at Woods Hole, on Massachusetts' Cape Cod, absorb the 99 per cent in less than 24 feet. By comparison with fresh water, this is still amazingly clear. The most transparent lake yet measured corresponds roughly to the turbidity at Woods Hole.

If the turbidity were uniform, only a ten-thousandth part of the light at the surface would penetrate to twice these depths. A ten-thousandth of full tropical sunshine at high noon is dim twilight indeed. A mere three-thousandth part is as bright to human eyes as a landscape under full moonlight—the limit of our ability to distinguish colors and see fine detail. In the ocean this level corresponds to 860 feet below the surface of the Sargasso Sea, or 40 feet at Woods Hole harbor.

William Beebe, dangling in his bathysphere off Bermuda, without artificial light could detect fish swimming by at most depths less than 2,000 feet—but not beyond. Along the Cape Cod coast this ultimate of night is less than 90 feet below the wave-skimming terns. Beyond these limits it makes no difference whether the sun is above the horizon or not; night is as eternal as the oceans.

Absence of light provides a real barrier in the sea. This is no simple choice between day-activity and nocturnality. The deeps are comparatively barren because aquatic plants—the basic food supply of the oceans—depend entirely on energy from the sun. Below an average depth of 250 feet, green plants cannot exist. Most sea life is limited to this surface layer—a mere 2 per cent of the total ocean volume. Under these creatures stretch abysses reaching almost six miles from sunlight.

Man's imagination has peopled the unknown abysses with monsters more terrible than real. Only when Britain became a sea power did the spirit of the deep acquire a more humorous mien—as good old Davy Jones. Often the ocean's bottom was the nearest land—the last resting place of dead ships—"Davy Jones' Locker." No one then had ever seen that lightless ocean floor. But a lead sinker weight could be greased on its blunt end and lowered on a rope to bring up a sample of the bottom. Coastal charts came to show not only the depths but also the underwater acres of stone, of sand, of many-colored muds. That a bottom "out of sight" could have this practical value in navigation led to even greater curiosity about deep water.

The angle between a sunbeam and the sea's surface has much to do with the depth to which daylight can penetrate, driving twilight and night to deeper levels. The higher the sun, the more directly does the energy enter, and the deeper it goes before being absorbed. Each day, as the sun rises above the oceans, arcs across the sky and sets again, each level of water above that with permanent night brightens and dims once more. In mid-March, night at the surface of Funchal harbor on the island of Madeira, near Gibraltar, lasts only 10 hours. At a depth of 66 feet, it continues for 13 hours.

At 100 feet, night takes up 19 hours. And at 133 feet, the water is blacked out for all but 15 minutes of a solar day— the brief span of dim twilight there.

In polar seas the abyssal night reaches far closer to the surface. At its highest point on a June noon, the sun is so low in the sky that day extends downward only shallowly. Yet only in waters illuminated by the sun can green plants thrive. There alone can sun energy be trapped and stored in molecules of sugars and starches, fats and proteins. There alone can microscopic plants nourish microscopic animals in enormous numbers, and these supply the food needs of larger crustaceans, of small fish and large, each in his turn. The year-long night pushes upward through polar oceans and so compresses the daylit waters that the fish are concentrated where diving sea birds can reach them. This nearness of night, even in the extended polar days of summer, explains in large part the tremendous throngs of gannets and gulls, puffins and penguins, auks and murres, that build their rookeries on craggy cliffs overhanging the cold seas.

As day reaches the upper waters, driving twilight deeper until the sun reaches the highest point in its arc through the sky, many animals adjust their position in the sea to remain on the dark fringe of the twilight zone. Some, like the little copepod crustacean *Calanus,* have developed a rhythmic habit of vertical migration which anticipates the changes in the sea above them. By day *Calanus* remains concentrated in the upper darkness, at a depth ranging from 1,100 to 1,500 feet. Toward sunset the various individuals begin swimming upward. Since the time of starting and speed of climb differ somewhat for each one, between 6 and 8 P.M. the population becomes distributed fairly evenly between 1,100 feet and the surface. By midnight all are browsing on green algae in the topmost 150 feet of ocean. Then down they go in a concerted rush that brings most of them, between 4 and 6 A.M., into the permanently lightless depths.

They seldom gain a glimmer of the sun energy their migrations avoid so regularly. Only a tardy *Calanus* may be stimulated by a twilight brightening of the sea around, and hasten downward to dark seclusion. The extent and speed of these migratory activities can be emphasized by comparing *Calanus* with a man. For the half-inch crustacean to travel up a thousand feet and down again each day, at half an inch each second, is equivalent to a man's dogtrotting for the same length of time at four miles an hour—covering 46 miles daily to reach a vegetable plate.

The number of sea animals performing these vertical migrations cannot be estimated. When electronic sound-producing devices were developed to replace the clumsy sounding line, measuring the distance to the bottom seemed easy. Depth could be calculated from the delay before a sharp pulse of sound waves beamed at the ocean's floor could echo back to special microphones. But frequently the sonar depth-recorder failed to confirm simultaneous findings with lead weight and line. Often sonar indicated shallower water at night than by day. A "phantom bottom" was reflecting the sound waves and providing the illusion.

151

To explain this phantom bottom, a "deep scattering layer" (abbreviated to DSL) was suggested. Extensive measurements accumulated. Only in the last few years, with explorations by French biologists in the underwater bathyscaphe, has the density of the living population of migrating small animals been realized. They form a "purée" of unbelievable congestion, crowded in the darkness—waiting to follow night into the rich pastures of green algae suspended in the water above.

Whether this concentration of animals provides the sonar echo is still a mystery. It seems illogical both that separate small individuals could yield so "solid" and "flat" an echo, and that so wonderful a banquet could be overlooked by all the fish that feed on the small animals—or by the squid which prey on the fish. It may well be that the echo is from squid and fish, but that these avoid all nets and cameras lowered to catch a record of their presence.

At night, when the migrant crustaceans rise to the surface waters and browse on the drifting, microscopic plant life there, fish and squid arrive in abundance. Schools of herring and other small fish sweep back and forth in such close ranks as to suggest a carpet in the water. Dogfish (small sharks) and seals rush in to catch a share, and the squid chase their victims with such abandon that they dart into the air. Night after night the *Kon-Tiki* was bombarded by these leaping squid. Some of the larger shrimp provide equally spectacular displays in darkness.

If, as a few oceanographers maintain, the DSL is a world-wide stratum of elusive squid, all waiting for night before rising toward the surface, then some of the questions concerning these animals have been solved. Squid must be prodigiously abundant, since they form the exclusive food (so far as known) of bottlenosed whales, and a major dietary item for sperm whales and other toothed whales, for seals while in the open ocean, and for sea birds of many kinds. Otherwise we have no hint as to where the squid stay from dawn to dusk—although their location must be close enough for the seals to swim to.

In their submarine dirigible, Houot and Willm settled freely to the sea's floor two and a half miles below their attending boats. All the way down their artificial lights showed them companion animals—six-foot sharks and two-inch hatchet fish, comb jellies and medusae, shrimps and prawns, and myriads of pea-sized crustaceans. At the greatest depth the bottom was pock-marked as though with gopher holes, where burrowing animals concealed themselves or tunneled in search of food. The quantity of life they found far exceeded all expectations. Below the twilight zones the animals must depend for food upon each other, plus the gentle rain of dead and dying, the carcasses, the crumbs and droppings that settle slowly through the darkness toward the bottom. Until recently the enormity of this food supply escaped man's understanding. The cold abyssal water even refrigerates this rain of oceanic manna on the way down!

Unending night stretches toward shore only because of the

greater turbidity of coastal water. Dissolved materials from the land fertilize the water, furnishing minerals upon which algal growth can bloom and support an increased population of alga-eating animals. This living contribution to the sea's turbidity is often overlooked, yet it is more significant than the coarser particles ground by wave action.

Around the rim of the earth's great continents, the oceans gnaw at lands projecting into the surf. Chunks of rock roll back and forth, ground by wave action into pebbles, into sand. Sand and flour-like muds slip away from the shoreline into deeper water, there to settle on earlier sediments as contributions to the continental shelves. These jutting shoulders extend often for many miles to sea, unmarked on most maps that show the familiar boundaries between land and ocean. Yet the continental shelves terminate with surprising uniformity wherever water covers them to a depth of an eighth of a mile—665 feet. There the land mass can truly be said to end.

Beyond the continental shelves the bottom is seldom sand or mud, and its nature is much more uniform than any soil exposed to air. Rocky bottoms are rare at these depths, and mark the path of deep rivers that scour their beds far below the ocean's surface, keeping them clean of any movable fragments. Elsewhere the floor is covered either by a great layer of soft ooze or by even greater thicknesses of firm red clay.

Red clay covers a larger area than any ooze. It is the typical deposit at the bottom of the Pacific Ocean, and is produced by decomposition of volcanic debris thrown into the air or washed into the erosive waves. Often it underlies immense populations of plants and animals which elsewhere would contribute continually to the bottom ooze. But at the depths where red clay is found, the water is under such tremendous pressure that limy and glassy shells dissolve before sinking all the way. Calcareous and silicious substances cannot exist there exposed in solid form.

Calcareous ooze covers nearly a third of ocean bottoms beyond the continental shelves. It is the usual deposit in tropical and subtropical waters, and consists of countless minute limy shells. In small areas and over relatively shallow regions, it may be the remains of swimming snails—the pteropods—which cavorted in the upper water, died and disintegrated, contributing their delicate internal shells to the ooze below.

Far more extensive in the darkness is calcareous ooze formed as accumulated shells of the single-celled animal *Globigerina*. These microscopic creatures build a spiral series of interconnected chambers, a curving row of annexes, each larger than the one before. From all the walls, long slender limy needles extend into the water. These serve both to hinder the sinking of *Globigerina* out of the lighted waters into the sunless depths of ocean, and also to support fingers of protoplasm reaching out into the sea for food of even smaller size.

Two very different types of life contribute the glassy matter in silicious ooze. One multitude is that of single-celled animals—the radiolarians—whose radiating network of needles and cross-members serve the protoplasm as does the limy skeleton of *Globigerina*. The other type is the myriad forms of diatoms—single-celled green plants dwelling in glass pill boxes of their own secretion—living and multiplying and dying, forever elaborating shells which settle downward to the bottom. Silicious ooze is most abundant in polar depths and in the ocean around the many islands of the East Indies. Like *Globigerina* ooze, it attests to the incredibly vast numbers of individual lives that have vanished, leaving behind only this microscopic skeletal trace. Yet the ooze is far from microscopic. It coats the ocean floor for thousands of square miles, to a depth of many feet. Estimates of the number of separate shells are as meaningless to our minds as the mileage to the farthest star.

In slow motion, soft-bodied sea cucumbers shove sticky tentacles before them into the inky bottom. One at a time the tentacles are thrust into the toothless mouth and sucked clean. Heart urchins progress inch by inch, half embedded, each one shoveling bottom particles into the mouth below, through the repeated dredging action of five converging teeth. Brittle starfish throw their slender arms into running waves that carry them slowly over the surface of the mud in a submarine counterpart of a sidewinding rattlesnake on desert sand.

As each animal advances, a diminutive pink "grass" of gill plumes vanishes abruptly into the ooze, each plume attached to the head end of a tunneling worm now retiring to subterranean safety. Burrowing clams withdraw their "necks" and for a time cease their exchange of old water for new, suspending feeding activities and figuratively holding their breath.

At intervals among this population of creeping and burrowing animals are other creatures more securely anchored. Sponges of many shapes spread upward, with porous bodies propelling water currents from which microscopic food can be extracted. Glass sponges, like the Venus' flower basket, attain engineering perfection in the depths. So, too, do the sea lilies. Each waves a flower-like body on the upper end of a long slender jointed stem rooted in the ooze. Great sea anemones, often crystal clear, sit on the bottom with their soft tentacles widely spread. Or the bottom may support a "meadow" of leathery, richly branching alcyonarian corals, a forest or a "moor" of taller sea fans—the gorgonians—each with its edge turned toward the source of a slow submarine current. From the branches of the alcyonarians, as from the flat surfaces of the gorgonian fans, small mouths project from short bodies bearing a ring of outstretched tentacles. Nettle cells on all these tentacles are perpetually ready to detect and capture small swimming animals as these accidentally brush against the trigger tips.

The delicacy of glass sponges, of sea-lily stems, of gorgonian fans, all show how ponderously gradual is any water movement in the depths. There are no tides, no waves, no sudden eddies. Even the crabs that stalk about among these deep-dwelling animals are often absurdly long-legged. They

157

are slender to the point of extreme fragility, as though fitted for tiptoeing over the soft felted floor of the sea. These crustaceans of the ocean bottoms are like giant counterparts of harvestman spiders on the land. Every country child has caught and held these harmless creatures, known as "daddy longlegs," and perhaps believed that they could point the direction toward errant cows.

By comparison with a harvestman, which can straddle three inches, an abyssal crab, stretching its legs five times as far, is huge. A few deep-sea crabs and fish grow to as much as three feet in length, some sharks to over six. But these are far less common than the minute animals of the ocean's floor. Even the hatchet fish, which appear so terrifyingly grotesque, gain their fearsomeness only when seen through a magnifier. Each extraordinarily wide mouth is set with fang-like sturdy teeth, and their stomachs are so distensible that they can hold prey larger than themselves. Yet two or three inches is their average length. Their lives are merely patterned on a different plan—depending on one or two opportunities a month to give them a stomach-filling meal, one large enough to last until the next chance.

Night in air has its glow-worms, its luminescing click beetles, and above all, its fireflies. The perpetual night of the abysses has an even greater variety of animals able to produce light, either continuously or, like fireflies, winking on and off. As a result, eyes still have value and degenerate blindness is far less common in the depths than in caves, where luminescent animals are so rare.

Even the bottom of the ocean contains oases of light. Alcyonarian meadows often glow with a soft continuous illumination against which swimming animals are silhouetted blackly. Forests of gorgonian fans irradiate the bottom avenues between the parallel rows of upright blades, like wafer-thin skyscrapers with lighted windows. The predominant color of this display is green, but patches of contrasting hues give evidence of still different kinds of bottom dwellers. Some worms creep exposed while aglow with red or purple light; others shine in orange or blue. Perhaps the luminescence attracts small animals which benefit the light-producer as food. But this explanation hardly applies to scavenging starfish which glide along, studding the ocean's bed with light.

Nearly half of the fish in the great depths produce light. Spots and streaks along their sides glow like the portholes and promenade decks of ocean liners. No doubt the pattern of these luminescent markings is highly useful in finding mates. It must serve also in detecting food or recognizing the approach of enemies. Often the light-producing organs are so well developed that each has a mirror backing and a superficial lens, concentrating the radiance into a definite direction. A few fish even have lid-like folds of the body skin, and can pull these through muscular contraction, to cover the luminescent organ in the deep-sea equivalent of a wink.

Wherever animal senses are strained to the limit by living conditions, a few kinds of creatures can usually be found in

which overdevelopment compensates in some measure for the feebleness of stimulation. This is noticeable particularly at the dark edge of the twilight zone in the sea, where squid of many sizes and a great variety of swimming crustaceans show tremendous expansion of the eyes. These organs bulge outward from the body, or occupy an unusually high percentage of the space available within the head. Often the eyes of deep-sea squid possess enormous lenses which collect the remnants of the sunlight reaching them; the proportions of the eye are so distorted that the term "telescopic eye" has been applied. Instead of a small lens through which adequate light can illuminate a large hemispheric retina, the huge lens collects the feeble light and concentrates it on a small circle of retina. As in a telescope the field of view is narrowed severely to include only a restricted angle toward which the eye is pointing.

Telescopic eyes are found in owls and in one nocturnal primate of the Philippines and Australasian islands—the tarsier. In all of these the visual organs are so huge that they cannot be moved in the head. Instead, the head as a whole is free to rotate through all 360 degrees, and binocular vision is usual. In deep-sea squids, by contrast, the telescopic eyes project from the body like gun turrets. They can be swiveled about in the dark water to aim at objects of interest. But apparently the eyes are independent and provide no binocular field and stereoscopic rangefinding.

Restriction of vision often leads to overdevelopment of other senses. Shrimp and prawns in the night of ocean deeps bear unusually long antennae—feelers three, eight, twelve times the length of their bodies. These sensitive extensions probe actively in all directions, ready to warn their wearers of danger before it comes too close. Fish commonly have fins modified into feelers longer than the body, and dart away when any object touches these outstretched organs. Stilt-like legs of abyssal crabs may serve the same function. Like antennae, they are expendible parts that can be cast off if seized. Later, each can be regenerated.

To the undersea explorer the animals seen through the portholes of a diving device appear silent. Yet even in darkness they can communicate by clicks and grunts conveyed by the surrounding water. No adequate study of this aspect of the deep sea has been attempted, but at lesser depths its counterpart is well known. Men with hydrophones, listening intently to amplified sounds from underwater for an approaching submarine, were treated often to false alarms when a school of fish or porpoise passed below. Apparently these swimmers maintain their group formation through sound signals. In shallow water the pistol shrimps snap their claws with force enough to stun small passing prey, or to break the glass wall of a light aquarium tank. These sounds in water close to the surface suggest what can be expected in the depths.

It seems strange that animals in perpetual night should have need for ways to disappear. Some of the shrimp discharge into the water a cloud of luminescent substances, using this technique to confuse a pursuing enemy. In the darkness the sudden burst of light may be matched by a dissolved chemical serving to stun the sense of taste. The bright cloud would then be equivalent to the fog of ink thrown out by a fleeing squid or octopus, for the "smoke screen" not only serves to end visual pursuit but also numbs the chemical senses of a pursuer.

Dark colors are valuable aids to disappearance even in the blackest water. They reflect little of the luminescence passing by, and give no cues to sensitive eyes. In the depths red is the most common hue. But since all of the long wavelengths of solar energy are absorbed within the topmost 165 feet of ocean, no light reaches a red animal that it can reflect. Until artificial light is introduced below this depth, red shrimp and fish are indistinguishable from the less frequent black ones. Short wavelengths too are unable to penetrate far into the sea. Dark violet animals and purple ones vanish as completely as do red or black.

Bluish green is the last remainder of daylight to be found in ocean depths. Here again the adaptations of animals afford cause to marvel. Not only are the creatures of the deep sea obviously recent migrants from its upper levels but their eyes, like those of men, show a clear relation to the uneven transparency of turbid water. In all eyes there must be a light-sensitive substance the bleaching of which starts off the chemical changes upon which vision depends. In order to be most efficient in sea water, this sensitive pigment should absorb energy maximally in the bluish green—allowing the eye to operate even at the fringe of darkness. Only one pigment is known to meet these specifications. After becoming familiar as "visual purple," it is now called rhodopsin. This substance is the hallmark of fish that lay their eggs in the sea, and of animals in whose remote ancestry the marine way of life was important; it is characteristic of the rod cells of reptiles, birds, and mammals. Closely allied is the pigment used by the great group of cephalopod mollusks: the octopus, squid, and cuttlefish—all of them marine.

A different pigment, porphyropsin, is present in rod cells of fish that spawn in fresh water, and of the tadpole stage of frogs. Its peak of absorption falls in the yellow-green, and matches better the wavelengths of the solar spectrum which penetrate deepest into lakes.

The black edge of twilight in deep water has left its mark upon all the animals with a camera type of eye. For eons this boundary must have held extreme importance for survival. In salt water or fresh the problem was essentially the same—night that recedes briefly into lower levels, only to rise again with the setting of the sun. The visual purple which lets men see at night is a badge of ancient comradeship with fish and squid. Like a heraldic coat-of-arms it is a symbol of our past association with the upper edge of sea-old night.

ELEVEN

Jungles under Moonlight

MIDNIGHT, deep in a tropical jungle, is darker than anywhere else on the surface of the earth. No light at all reaches the soil even under the brightest stars. The most sensitive photographic film could be exposed for hours without fogging. Eyes are of no use whatever. Yet in this blackness live more kinds of plants, and among them more types of animals, than anywhere else in the world.

The wealth of jungle life is so well known that when a naturalist arrives in the tropics and visits a rain forest, he expects to find the richness of a zoological park set in a botanical garden. He is seldom warned that of each kind of creature, the total number of individuals is far smaller than in any temperate woods. Nor does he realize how expertly the animals keep out of one another's way—and out of human sight. Most of them are strictly nocturnal, and wary even then. As a result, the rain forest floor gives a sense of empty finality. Nothing seems to happen. The lack of leaves within reach is matched by a lack of breeze to make them flutter. Even by day few birds fly through the dim aisles, and few sounds reach the ear except the timeless drip of moisture from downhanging vines or the accidental crash of a rotted limb. Other than ants, few insects crawl about. Even the ants act as though they were in constant fear of getting lost. They move quietly in single file, or scour the jungle litter in raiding parties whose individuals keep within sight of one another.

So inconspicuous are the jungle animals that the vegetation seems overwhelming. After forty years of directing scientific studies in the tropics, William Beebe concluded that "it is the silent, terrible warfare of the plant world which is most impressive. A great tree at the trailside, perhaps two centuries from saplinghood, is being strangled by the snake-like coils of a huge liana or climbing vine, and not only by constriction but by smothering."

The scattering of fallen leaves and fading petals gives scant clue to the trees above. "It is next to impossible to look up and determine with certainty which leaves belong to a particular tree. The confusion of interlacing branches is complete, and a tree which bears, say, three tons of leaves may . . . support five tons of epiphytes ranging in bulk from microscopic algae, tiny mosses, and half-inch orchids to enormous, thick-leaved, woody parasites, one individual of which may replace a third or even half of the original tree crown."

166

These differences from the temperate zone are so striking that everyone interested in living things should find an opportunity to experience a jungle. Some years ago the plant explorer David Fairchild chided us gently: "You live in New England. Don't you know that's the *fringe* of the world? Most of the really interesting and unusual plants, and the strangest of all animals, inhabit the torrid zone. Get to the tropics and see for yourselves. Don't say you can't afford the travel costs. Whenever a small boy tells me he can't save enough money to go to the circus, I know he doesn't want to go badly enough!"

So we went to the tropics, and chose for our initiation the relatively safe though dense jungles of Panamá. On a sanctuary island only three miles across, we each carried a whistle by day, a whistle and a flashlight by night. One of us stayed on the trail whenever the other deviated into "the bush."

The naturalist Bates expressed a "feeling of inhospitable wildness" in the rain forests of the Amazon basin, and Charles Darwin reached the same conclusion elsewhere in South America. Tomlinson found the jungle "securely aloof and indifferent" to the point of impartial hostility.

Even the man-hewn trails were unlike any we had met before. Indian-style, they ran from one high point to the next, rather than following any contour line. At the brink of a V-shaped valley, they descended directly and went straight up the other wall. With the temperature high and humidity so great that sweat rolled off without evaporating, even a mile of trail presented a challenge. Intermittent rains kept the mud below our feet wet and slippery.

Robert Louis Stevenson wrote of the jungle that "a man can see to the end of nothing; whichever way he looks the wood shuts up, one bough folding with another like the fingers of your hand." We found this true enough at the borders or overhead. But once through the barrier at the water's edge, really tangled jungle proved to be far more local than we had anticipated. For the most part, a mature tropical rain forest is as open at the bottom as is a dense stand of California redwoods. So little light reaches the ground by day that seedlings have no chance. High humidity and temperature encourage the decomposing action of molds and bacteria. In a few short weeks fallen leaves and branches vanish, adding nothing to the soil. "Soil" of the sort that an Iowa farmer would recognize is absent altogether. The regular rains leach out soluble minerals. No humus accumulates. Instead the jungle floor is a naked mud on which a few bits of plant debris lie loosely in varying stages of rapid decay.

Moving slowly along the ground at any hour of the twenty-four, man is a Lilliputian captive of gravity. Around him crowd upright boles and a warp of sinewy lianas stretching from the ground to the leafy canopy above. It is as though the jungle foliage were a dense green cloud tethered to the earth by pendant vines, and pierced at many points by the smooth trunks of giant trees.

All the world seems inaccessible and hidden from view.

For forty or fifty feet straight up, the trunks neither fork nor bear a leaf. Then the tree tops visible from the ground send out horizontal limbs from which extend almost vertical branches. On these the greenery is borne—spread out flatly like flowers of wild parsley or Queen Anne's lace. Yet this is merely the understory of foliage. Above it, tier on tier, are other levels to heights of a hundred or a hundred and fifty feet. Over this, again, tower the real giants such as *Bombacopsis,* thrusting their crowns skyward two hundred feet or more. All nature seems arboreal. The daytime birds, the flowers, the butterflies, are on the top. A person walking on the jungle floor is as isolated from their world as a worm crawling over the sand below a beachside boardwalk.

Unlike a temperate forest, where the dominant trees may be beech or oak or pine, the jungle includes no solid stands. An almendro tree here, a roble there, a silk-cotton (*Cieba*) just beyond. The next almendro may be half a mile away. Only when the tree-buttercups (*Tabebuia*) flaunt their waxy gold blossoms toward the sun can a census taker in an airplane count the separate similar trees in a square mile of bush.

Time in the jungle follows a special rhythm. The tick of the clock is the call of birds, of frogs and toads, of katydids. It is the whine of cicadas, the swish of swaying branches, the patter of feet on leaves, the pelt of down-pouring rain. Its rhythm is syncopated, with pauses full of silence. From eight in the morning until five in the afternoon, most animals are asleep. But as the burning sun slides toward the horizon,

the nocturnal world responds to the approach of night. Butterflies and bees which have been busy on the jungle roof descend into the shadows and find familiar sleeping sites. Birds which were silent through the sunny hours take a new and active interest in their twiglit surroundings. Gaily colored toucans flit from the leafy depths to upper limbs, then take off for some bare branch which commands the scene. The rapid flight, with long undulating course, displays the slender, crow-sized body and big bright beak held straight ahead.

Two toucans per dead tree seems to be the jungle rule. They perch facing one another in the sunset, a few feet apart, lifting their yellow-mottled bills into the air to yelp out strangely unbirdlike calls: Hí—kyuck, kyuck. Hí—kyuck, kyuck.

Late one afternoon we watched a pair of black spots against the flaming sky become a twosome of Amazona parrots, stout green birds which flap short wings as vigorously as any duck. They approached in a wide arc and settled in the same dead stub as two toucans. Throughout their heavy flight the parrots screamed to one another in short rasping syllables. Now on the tree they faced the black-bodied toucans and screeched defiantly. The toucans yelped back. At the outset, the parrots sounded hoarse. But in this contest they had the advantage in volume, though the toucan calls rang through the jungle, clear and loud.

As the sunset colors faded a dozen parakeets rose in a cloud and circled over the parrot-toucan contestants. The smaller green birds added to the uproar with a chatter of sound. The parrots leaped from their perches and flapped off across the clearing, only a few wing-beats ahead of the parakeets. Behind them on the dead stub, the toucans continued a few victorious yelps, then lapsed into silence. Soon, with a whirr of wings, they too departed. A big red-crested woodpecker swooped in, following a course with shorter undulations and comparative quiet. It alighted on the dead stub and set up a tattoo of drumming in short bursts. The pitch varied as the bird shifted around the trunk. Finally it settled in one place where the note had a particularly deep resonance. Suddenly the sound ceased, and the woodpecker flew away into the gathering darkness.

By six in a July evening, human eyes could distinguish few hues. But hummingbirds produced a fluffy whirr as they

171

darted from one blossom to another, hurrying to fill each crop with sugar water before night ended their feeding. From the colonnade of tree trunks came an occasional whine from a cicada—a long steady buzz which might deepen as though to run down, then rise again. The note would coast almost to a stop, pick up sharply, coast once more, and finally die altogether.

Exactly at six thirty, night after night, we heard from the jungle a firm, flutelike whistle, followed by another in tremolo half a tone higher. A big, grouselike tinamou had begun the nocturnal serenade. Between two outflung buttresses of a *Bombacopsis* tree she had laid four turquoise-blue eggs in a close cluster. Now her mate—a smaller, quieter bird—was incubating them, and would continue alone at this task until they hatched and he had raised the chicks to independence. Her calls in the jungle were a summons for another unattached male. The sweet, sad cadence came deliberately, with exquisite timing; we never could hear a male reply. Visual confirmation seemed impossible. So rarely can any jungle singer be seen that Beebe considered having a rubber stamp made to use daily in his diary: "The leaves moved but I could not see a bird."

Usually the tinamou was joined audibly by others in the distance, each vocally staking out ownership of a patch of darkening jungle. A large cicada set up a whine with a rapidly rising and falling note, repeated over and over. A big tree frog began a birdlike churring, while from all directions came short staccato peepings of smaller amphibians. In the water-filled cavity of a five-foot stump left by the fall of an almendro tree, several small toads began a chorus. They were passing air from mouth to oversized sacs behind their ears, fretting their vocal cords into an uneven bellow-and-chirp that included a dry rattling sound and that of a plucked reed.

By six fifty the katydids were replacing the cicadas, filling in the gaps between the full-throated whistling of the tinamous. The inch-long toads in the stump pond had reached a peak of volume, and a flashlight revealed them—whipping the water to a froth with their exhaled breath. Each toad was behind a little heap of brown suds.

After seven o'clock the night activities of jungle animals were in full swing. Now the climbing creatures had fewer enemies, and they traveled aloft to gather nuts and fruits. Occasionally an owl sailed by, but no eagles, falcons, or

173

hawks disturbed the foraging of monkeys and honeybears (kinkajous).

Like the tree porcupines, the silky anteaters ripping open termite nests (and the opossums, monkeys, and honeybears) have a fifth hand to help them hold their place—a long prehensile tail which can be curled around a branch.

Slower-moving foliage-eaters clamber about in the tree tops. Giant lizards—the green iguanas—stretch their six-foot length over the firm jungle covering of interlacing vines, to munch on buds and fresh leaves. Each is ready at a moment's notice to leap from the tree and crash to the ground. There the lizard scampers off, or, falling in any shallow waterway, hides in the bottom, waiting for a pursuer to give up the chase.

By contrast, the sloths feeding in the treetops cling to the branches below, from which they are suspended by hooked claws. These slowest of all mammals prefer the broad, many-fingered foliage of the *Cecropia,* a member of the mulberry family common throughout the American tropics but found nowhere else. Apparently their thick matted fur protects them from the hordes of small brown ants which make homes far from the ground in the hollow stems of this tree and attack any intruder.

On the soil far below the sloths, larger ants forage ceaselessly all day. Systematically they explore every log and leaf and cranny, seizing any form of living meat—whether mouse or bird, lizard or frog, grasshopper or spider. They tear apart each victim and distribute its remains as loads of flesh to be carried back along the column—nourishment to be shared with the brood of young carried by still other members of the colony. These are the dreaded army ants—the American *Eciton*—which resemble in their habits the driver ants of tropical Africa. But like old-time armies which fought by day and slept at night, these terrors of the rain forest respond to a silent, military tattoo at sunset. The columns cease their ad-

vance. The marching order is reversed. From everywhere the ants converge on a central rendezvous. And as the light fails, some inaudible signal leads these insects to climb a low bush or some strong liana to a point several feet above the ground. There they mass themselves into a tremendous quivering ball. Until daybreak this bivouac will cling together as a unit, ready to unfold, when morning comes, into a dozen raiding parties and a wholesale transportation system.

Other ants parade up and down a variety of trees. In the

night they are safe from ant shrikes, honeycreepers, and other insect-eating birds. Sauba ants, known also as parasol or umbrella ants, climb to reach fresh foliage, choosing chiefly trees which are exceptional in the tropics in having small, thin leaves. Each half-inch ant employs one of its sidewise-working slender jaws to saw off an arc of leaf blade, handling the knife edge with the precision of a surgeon. Dexterous movements of all six legs transfer the fragment to the paired jaws, and the insect marches off with its booty held above its back like a green sail. Often whole petals are carried along in this fashion.

As the stevedores plod down the tree, they blunder every few steps into eager ants returning for another load. The two-way column wanders along the ground, converging with other living streams upon an irregular mound many feet across—the granular earth excavated from deep subterranean burrows. Down the many doorways the insects descend to transfer their burdens to still smaller sisters who drag the booty to chambers as large as bushel baskets. There the small ants mince the leaf pieces into a pulp.

Sauba ants are the agriculturalists of the tropical jungle. "In addition, they are the greatest defoliators known, their ravages far exceeding those of other famous leaf destroyers such as the Japanese beetle and the gypsy moth." All of their activities lead to the building of vast compost heaps in which strands of a particular kind of fungus grow. So far as is known the sauba ants eat nothing but this fungus, and they alone have the secret of its culture. When a young queen ant starts out to found a fresh colony, she carries with her a pellet of the fungus and tends it carefully until her first brood of young emerge.

Fortunately the sauba ants do not bite, and an explorer of the jungle night who stands unwittingly across their trail suffers no ill effects. By day their paths are clearly visible—little avenues four to seven inches broad, kept remarkably clear of sticks and stones, patted firm by myriad marching feet.

Far more irregular and plastic are the tracks of wild pigs—peccaries—whose sharp toes dig into the wet earth, and whose noses root vigorously in search of hidden food.

During nights in January, February, and early March these and other animals are particularly active under the spreading branches of great almendro trees. At this season the flattened elliptical nuts are ripening—each about two inches long and one inch wide. The brown outer covering has a slightly sweetish taste and is attractive to raccoon-like coatis and to howler monkeys by day, to honeybears by night. Inside the skin, however, is a layer hard as stone, protecting the almond-shaped inner kernel for which the tree is named —even though it is a member of the pea family. The honey-bears and monkeys pick the fruit, eat off the outer coat, and drop the shell-bound kernels. Waiting for this bounty, on the ground below are herds of white-lipped peccaries. A man needs a sledge-hammer to break the covering. Rabbit-like agoutis and squirrels gnaw through the hard shell. "The peccary, on the other hand, cracks the nut along the lateral seam that divides it into halves, a tribute to the hardness of his teeth and the power of his jaws."

Of all the known terrors in a jungle night, none compares with a herd of white-lipped peccaries. High boots and loose trousers can be worn as protection against poisonous snakes, and antivenins are available if one is bitten in spite of precautions. But "in the presence of a large herd of peccaries all of which rush viciously to the attack, a man, no matter how carefully chosen his arsenal, would have just about as much chance of coming off unscathed as a lightning beetle attacked by a regiment of army ants." Their armament is a pair of razor-sharp tusks in each jaw—weapons with which they slash an enemy to pieces.

These white-lipped wild pigs are frequently nocturnal and travel several abreast in bands of fifty to a hundred. Each adult animal weighs about a hundred pounds, and can demonstrate remarkable speed in either escape or attack. They are far more formidable than the collared peccaries which often scavenge the same jungle. The collared pigs are a third smaller, less odoriferous, form bands of eight or ten, and trot through the rain forest in single file. Tapir and deer, which pay no attention to the collared peccary, usually desert a region as soon as a band of white-lips moves in. Man must travel carefully in their neighborhood for, although they usually run off to avoid a meeting, they sometimes choose to charge, and do so with a terrifying clattering of teeth like "hundreds of castanets." The only haven from

attack is in a tree. And smooth, branchless jungle trees are notoriously hard to climb.

The nearness of white-lipped peccaries is usually obvious to one's nose, since their musk is powerful and clings to the ground in the hothouse air of a jungle night. Eyes, however, seem more reliable. If for no other reason, the most stout-hearted night explorer of a jungle trail may be reluctant to turn off his flashlight and depend alone on his nose and ears. Often the patch of brightened area seems all too small. A soft-treading puma or a spotted jaguar could easily be preparing to pounce from the blind rear. A constrictor snake might be looped from the next low limb—a thirty-foot anaconda or a twelve-foot boa. How many six-inch tarantulas are waiting along the trail, crouching at the mouths of their down-slanted burrows?

These animals seldom attack a man, but in the pitch blackness of the rain forest, statistics offer a puny shield! Although we knew how acoustically dead the tropical woodland was, it seemed that our stumbling steps must alert every creature within a radius of a mile. Perhaps it would be better to sit quietly on an ant-free log, and wait for some animal to become curious enough to approach. Then right behind us a limb would crash, tearing leaves from branches and branches from trees. Fungus and ter-mites had done their work, digesting dead wood and re-turning part of a tree to its mother earth.

On one night, our confidence high, we sat resolutely on a stump with flashlights off, listening to the squeaks and twitterings in the foliage high overhead. Suddenly, something snorted and brushed an outstretched foot. Startled, we pressed our lamp switches and found ourselves facing a pair of quarter-ton tapirs. They were as startled as we. Down the trail they bolted, snorting, their broad backs wet and glistening. This largest animal native to Central and South America is a relative of the rhinoceros, but its flexible nose extends three or four inches as a soft proboscis which can be moved in all directions. Normally it hangs down over the mouth "like a drooping eyelid," but when frightened, the myopic mammal twists it from side to side and up and down, snorting and sniffing, apparently deciding which way to dash next.

Night still affords advantages not offered by day. For we barely glimpsed the brown bird which quietly vacated a pendant nest hung on the tip of a low palm leaf. Was it the large hummingbird known as a "Nicaraguan hermit"? In the dim afternoon light filtering through the ocean of leaves above us, no markings seemed distinctive as she flew. Yet after dark, when we returned, the mother sat as for her portrait, with only a bright eye cocked in our direction. We made a photograph of her from a distance of no more than ten feet. The flash bulb blazed, the shutter clicked, but the Nicaraguan hermit moved not a single feather. Whether in jungle or temperate forest, birds are reluctant to leave their nests at night, and pictures of them incubating their eggs are particularly easy to get.

Any field trip in the jungle night involves calculated

hazards. If we dozed while sitting without a light, a hungry vampire might take advantage. We would miss seeing the specialist at work—opening a painless wound with razor-sharp teeth, and lapping the blood without disturbing the sleeper. A light will fend them off and so will movement. So long as we moved along the trail or kept a lamp burning, we had no need to fear them. Nor, in the wilder jungles of Guiana, was Beebe "conscious of the bloody fang, the poison tooth, of the wilderness. The peace of this jungle at night was the same peace as that of the trees in our city parks."

Even with a reliable flashlamp and no rain, events in a jungle night can be unpredictable. We found a brook less precipitous than most—one with permanent pools which cascaded gently down a slope. Time and again we visited the place a few hours after sunset, to watch the fresh-water shrimp sculling around, their big stalked eyes aglow with a reddish fire. If we stood downstream and held the light low, they would approach us, burning brilliantly by reflected eyeshine. On one of these occasions, while we were concentrating on shrimp, a wild yell cut through the darkness— probably the death scream of a coati which had been pounced upon by a jungle cat. Instantly the birds above awoke and began to clamor. In the topmost boughs a troupe of howler monkeys took up the cry with a crescendo of coughing barks that merged into one appalling roar, an "endless earth-shaking moan, followed by a quick series of grunts like staccato thunder." How many of the monkey tribe contributed to the hullabaloo we could not tell. But Bates, who commented on how much the howlers "deepened the feeling of solitude which crept on as darkness closed around us," was indulging in British understatement when he wrote that it is "a most fearful and harrowing noise, under which it is difficult to keep up one's buoyancy of spirit."

The chorusing of howler monkeys can begin at any time of night. Usually they are heard by day. A thunderstorm will start them, and the claps of exploding air are dimmed by the primate cries. "If contests were held among the beasts of the world to determine the one with the most powerful voice, the howling monkey would certainly be acclaimed champion on every occasion—the roar of the lion, the howl of the wolf, even the wail of a banshee dwindling to a mere whisper beside the efforts of the great, bearded vocalist of the South [and Central] American forests." Yet this is the sound of a jungle dawn. There is no cheerful chirruping of robins, as on a temperate lawn, welcoming the new day. Night surrenders above a tropical forest to the reverberating jeers and hoots of this Stentor among mammals—to a skirl of defiance which ends human sleep more effectively than any alarm clock.

TWELVE

Polar Darkness

WHETHER a zebra is black with gray stripes or gray with black markings depends upon the point of view. Similarly the polar lands can be described as those the sun deserts completely once a year or as those whose otherwise continuous night is infringed by an annual tide-like encroachment of day. The blue skies and warmth of arctic summer tend to conceal the fact that only from the sun come enough radiations to make life possible in a polar night. Stars are present in every month. So little of their heat arrives as to be negligible; and their light is so dim that by night the portion of their energy scattered by the earth's atmosphere is too scant for eyes to detect.

It is tempting to assume that less night, more heat, is all the arctic needs to become a garden paradise. Yet if rain and snowfall remained as they are at present, a little more warmth would turn the great tundra lands into the largest desert on earth. Only the cold of polar darkness keeps the soil so frozen that drainage is blocked, making the "Dreaded Barrens" a summer patchwork of lakes and bogs. Few indeed are the polar rivers that flow to the sea.

The southern limit of treeless tundra is the 50-degree isotherm for the warmest month. This irregular line bounds bleak land which never fully loses its frost in summer. Below the tundra surface is "permafrost"—soil which has been frozen ever since glaciers covered so much of North America and Europe. At Fairbanks, Alaska, it extends 170 feet below anything the sun can thaw. At Amderma, on the north coast of Siberia, it continues downward for 1,200 feet.

The area of this frozen land is far from negligible. A twentieth of the earth's surface—all of it in the northern hemisphere—is tundra. No tree can find space for roots in the shallow summer mud except along the scarce, meandering rivers; there, alders and low willows thrive. Elsewhere the bogs are full of peat moss (sphagnum) and various sedges, especially the great tufts of cottongrass. Lemmings and mice build their runways. Land elevated a foot or two above summer water level grows grasses, marmots, and ground squirrels. Everywhere, from bare rock to soggy sphagnum, lichens flourish—evidently the hardiest plants of all.

In temperate lands, lichens rate so low in the dietary preferences of animals as to be almost free from attack. In an arctic night they form the staple food for lemming and caribou, and often allow a hungry bear to survive a temporary scarcity of other kinds of nourishment. So regularly do those roaming deer, the caribou, feed on lichens, that one gray shrubby type is known as "reindeer moss" even far to the south.

Over a major part of the tundra, night is complete in December and January. Neither sun nor obvious twilight brightens the sky. Yet winter is dark, not black. The snow-covered landscape reflects starshine, and "northern lights" may glow overhead. Sometimes the aurora borealis appears as great luminous clouds which blink on and off. Or rippling arcs and streamers may fan out from the horizon like search-lights. Often the effect is of a broad, fluted curtain across a gigantic stage. Its color can be greenish yellow, edged at the bottom with red. Frequently the streamers are blue or violet or gray or orange-red.

Science has not yet learned which of several theories most adequately explains the aurora. To the ancient Norsemen the display was reflections from the shining shields of Valkyries bearing to Valhalla the heroes slain in battle. This view is certainly more poetic than that which ascribes it to excited molecules of nitrogen (luminous in orange-red, blue-green, blue-violet and deep violet) and oxygen (red and chartreuse) in the upper atmosphere.

Except for the wind, a polar night is usually quiet. Soli-tude becomes impressive but not depressing. In the compara-tive calm between storms, the stars glow brightly, the auro-ral pageant is ever fresh. All the world seems clean. There is a continual temptation to stand and stare at the whiteness extending from the sea to the summit of a distant peak. Then it is that the human ear picks up the high-pitched call of a wolf "singing the beauty of the night, singing it as no human voice [has] ever done, calling on a mate to share the beauty of it with him . . . like a breath of wind, rising slowly, softly, clearly to a high, lovely note of sadness and longing; dying down on two distinct notes so low that . . . human ears [can] scarcely catch them."

The total disappearance of the sun in polar winter is accompanied by another phenomenon scarcely less spectacular. The full moon remains above the horizon constantly, circling the sky. The moon's orbit is inclined to that of the earth (the ecliptic) just enough (five degrees) to prevent a monthly eclipse of the sun on the one hand and of the moon on the other. As a result, when the sun rises and sets progressively farther to the south in fall, the moon rises and sets correspondingly more to the north. Finally the sun vanishes for everyone who lives above the Arctic Circle. The full moon is left beaming continuously upon the frozen land.

The depth of polar snow is usually overestimated. It seems so logical that the film of whiteness in Arizona or Virginia, growing to many feet in Wyoming or New Hampshire, should be part of a graduated snowbank totalling hundreds of feet in thickness on Greenland's ice cap and over the frozen wastes of polar America. But actually a New England ski slope or a Wyoming valley provides far more winter cover for vegetation than does a tundra plain. The essential aridity of the far north is much too real. The frozen soil is "physiologically dry" to the plants in that they can take no moisture from it most of the year. In addition, the snowfall is light—not much more than enough to insure that all of the level ground will stay covered in spite of gales.

Probably the real reason that caribou migrate southward in growing darkness, to spend winter south of the tundra among the evergreen fringes of northern woods, is a need to escape the wind. Muskox, with their long shaggy coats, seem impervious as they munch on grasses reached through the snow or willows along a water course. Moose stick to the willows and alders, perhaps gaining some protection from the low bare trees.

Almost all the summer birds fly south, many of them tremendously far. Snow buntings may remain among the nearest solid stand of trees or migrate into the northern states if a supply of seeds and berries cannot be found with less traveling. Ptarmigan change color, from summer brown to winter white, with transitional stages still matching the patches of snow and bare ground. Their diet requires slight southward movement—to regions where they can find winter buds of alder and birch, poplar and willow. Flocks of these grouse-sized birds often plunge headlong into soft snow to rest concealed all night. But tundra winds tend to pack the snow too tightly, and effectively shut them out. In the shelter of trees the gales are mollified and snow retains its lightness longer.

When the winter-long night arrives, it finds many arctic creatures in new fur coats which match the snow. Lemmings no longer appear to be plain meadow mice. The arctic hare and the arctic fox transform like the weasel to ermine-white. Against the snow-covered landscape they are almost invisible. The hare crouches with its golden eyes nearly closed, its black-tipped ears laid backward, and rests, secure in its white garb. When the hare blends with the white monotone of winter, not even a shadow is likely to give it away. If the sun comes above the horizon for a few hours around noon, fogs and mists are likely to rise, providing a protecting shroud. Even its timidity vanishes to the degree that a person can approach and seize it bare-handed. In summer, by contrast, the same animal is briefly brown and wary for all three months.

A good many animals in a polar night change their habits and become hoarders. Arctic foxes collect all the ptarmigan they can catch and bury them in the snow toward a future time of hunger. The arctic wolf, which stays white all year, caches whatever meat cannot be eaten on the spot.

Searching for the food stores laid away by lesser animals becomes a profitable occupation. The rodents are most often robbed. Lemmings, which, in fall, extend their straw-lined burrows where they will be covered by firm snow, accumulate rootlets toward the lean days of darkness. Mice, especially the red-backed, garner seeds and dry fruits. Even the shrews, which in summer are at least 50 per cent insectivorous, build stockpiles of vegetation for consumption in the cold. Wolf and fox and bears (both grizzly and polar) hunt out these provident animals, and thereby gain both fresh

meat and the food capital each has saved. Lemmings, as the most numerous of these smaller creatures, actually furnish the food base for man's fur trade. They are also the "most joyous feature" of the tundra in all seasons, as they frisk about, popping in and out of their branching burrows.

Snowy owls, which remain white in every month, wear feathers even on their feet—good insulation against the cold surfaces on which they stand while waiting for an opportunity to catch lemmings and other small mammals. These birds dive for their prey from well overhead, and can be foiled through a simple expedient. The intended victim need only crouch among boulders or below an overhanging snowdrift to be immune. Neither the snowy owl nor its less common relative, the gray owl, seems to know how to walk along the ground to follow prey.

So largely do the owls and foxes in particular depend upon lemmings that any major change in the numbers of the lichen-eaters alters living conditions for the predators. Foxes die out. Snowy owls migrate southward, occasionally as far as Florida, when the lemming supply falls off. Records of the Audubon Society indicates an exodus of snowy owls every four years since Christmas of 1926, except in 1937–38, when the interval was but three years.

Arctic hares may be second only to lemmings as a meat supply for fox and wolf, grizzly and lynx, weasel and owl. By preference they keep to slopes and ridges, where their racing progress uphill quickly discourages a pursuer on the surface. The hares detect food through a foot or two of snow, and use their powerful hind feet to break the crust, letting them tunnel downward to reach willow buds, bark, twigs, and bits of root which can be pulled free. Those animals which are driven to the coast by unusually heavy snow browse side by side with caribou on seaweeds cast ashore by storms. At these times the grizzlies and polar bears may join the hares, and all behave as peaceful vegetarians.

The weeks of winter darkness and the months of spring and fall when the sun stays briefly above the horizon provide an annual testing time for the highly adapted elite of polar lands. No mammal there can truly hibernate. Those which remain survive until summer because of the versatility of their dietary requirements and their tolerance of cold. Before them stretches a season of melted snow and ice, of suddenly abundant food, of migrant birds and multitudinous insects, of brilliant flowers on scrubby plants with leaves like leather, of fruits and seeds. Birds which have wintered in the tropics, competing there with a full complement of local creatures, flock to springtime in the tundras.

As night retreats, all the larger animals take advantage of the plants and of the insects which feed upon them. New broods are reared. Predators enjoy so many field days one after another that they stroll about satiated. Many potential victims show no fear whatever. Temporarily winter has relented. Compared to its rigors, living enemies are of little consequence. Reproduction is so prolific that almost every kind present includes many individuals which can be expended without endangering the survival of the species.

How unlike the tropics this situation is! There the weather is so uniformly beneficent that few die from its vagaries. Instead the living space is vigorously contested. Each animal specializes in self-effacement, in finding some few hours of the day wherein, for a few weeks at least, it can be active in feeding and reproducing without overwhelming competition. Social relations reach maximum complexity in a jungle. On the tundra they seem scarcely to exist.

Even the arctic plants show how unique are the conditions of existence in polar regions. Practically no plants there have thorns. Parasitic plants and those which, like fungi, feed on the decaying remains of woody growth are absent or rare.

Few climb on one another. Most are perennial, flowering year after year, perhaps because pollination is uncertain, perhaps because the survival of fruits and seeds over the winter is unlikely in the face of hungry mice and lemmings, caribou and muskox. A good many polar plants give their offspring an extra boost—holding them until the seedlings sprout before freeing them for dissemination.

The changing length of polar night leads the birds north, then drives them south again. Long before the airplane had been invented, the migrating birds showed up the unimportance of national boundaries. As darkness yields to day, spring thaws start the geese toward their breeding grounds. Through their flight "the waste corn of Illinois is carried through the clouds to the Arctic tundras, there to combine with the waste sunlight of a nightless June to grow goslings for all the lands between. And in this annual barter of food for light, and winter warmth for summer solitude, the whole continent receives as net profit a wild poem dropped from the murky skies upon the muds of March."

The tilt of the earth's axis and the bulge of the planet's spheroidal bulk conspire to give polar lands every possible variation in length of night, thereby restricting the kinds of life that can exist in arctic latitudes. For every sunless December day at the North Pole there is another in June over the antarctic continent. Yet the full moon which shines continuously above the South Pole brightens a night which is dead and empty. Instead of tundra full of activity, the antarctic is frozen mountains and high plateaus. Even the flightless penguins swim away from those shores when night is long.

Arctic areas are interpersed with waters of the sea and consequently there is never so large a drop in temperature as in areas many miles inland, toward the equator. Along the coasts, bordering the Arctic Ocean and its connections to warmer seas, men can subsist on seal and walrus, polar bear, and herds of caribou. Holes remain through the ice and permit the aquatic mammals to dive for food all winter long: the seals for fish and crustaceans, the walrus for mollusks that they can grub from the bottom with their curved tusks. No counterpart of these creatures spends winter in the antarctic. No man stands to admire and no wolf sings under the "southern light"—the aurora australis.

THIRTEEN

The Desert Night

NOWHERE in the world does sundown release so many animals from burrows as in a desert. Since early morning they have sought subterranean sanctuary from the burning glare. In twilight and darkness they emerge, detecting promptly the time when, through the clear air, the soil's surface has radiated to space enough of the excessive daytime heat. Their well-guarded store of water no longer is in such peril. Each can seek to supplement its energy supply, to find its favorite food.

Every desert-dwelling animal has some artful dodge whereby it can exist without liquid water from one year's end to the next. A few, like snails and frogs, wait underground not only from dawn to dusk but from one rain to the next, though the rains be a year apart. The rest depend on some special means for getting water. Most take it second

hand from the storage reservoirs of plants. Others manu-
facture the simple essential water molecule from atoms
gained in dry foods. Some subsist on smaller animals which
have these specific abilities.

Since almost three-fourths of the earth's surface is open
water—oceans, lakes, and rivers—it seems scarcely reasonable
that any land should be so dry. Yet of the total area of the
continents, more than a twelfth is desert, where the annual
rainfall rarely reaches as much as ten inches. Sometimes a
whole year goes by with no rain at all. Little or no subsur-
face water can be reached, and plants must either hoard
moisture from one shower to another, or remain dormant for
many months, even years.

The critical problem is always water. In the intense light
of day, a small area of green plant can capture all the sun
energy needed since the rate of growth is so limited by
drought. Any excess of surface above ground invites extra loss
of moisture. In consequence, the plants of the desert are
largely hidden. Enormous root systems, specialized for stor-
ing water and for capturing any that may sink in after a rain,
spread out in all directions and meet their neighbors. Exposed
to air may be only low woody shrubs, each separated widely
from the next by areas of naked soil.

To wander on foot through a desert, particularly after
dark, is to sense the uniqueness of living conditions there.
In the cactus forests of Arizona, on a night-time stroll with
naturalist-philosopher Joseph Wood Krutch and William
Woodin III of the Desert Museum in Tucson, we threaded

197

our way between prickly pear and barrel cactus, past waist-high chollas and clumps of eight-foot catclaw wands. At intervals a giant saguaro was silhouetted against the sky. Some of them rose as much as thirty feet from the desert floor, their spine-set accordion pleats imprisoning six to seven tons of water. Their blunt, curved branches suggest grotesque arms, somehow frozen by the heat in the middle of a gesture. Even these monster green reservoirs do not dispel the feeling that all vegetation in the desert grows low, grows spines, grows slowly.

In the side of many a saguaro, a circular hole can be seen —the doorway to the cactus woodpecker's flask-shaped nest. These birds hollow out a cavity from the soft wet heart of the plant, and wait until scar tissue seals the surface with a firm liner. Year after year the flicker-sized woodpecker may nest in the same place. Eventually the hole goes vacant. A diminutive squatter, the elf owl, moves in and takes advantage of the cavity.

It was this new tenant that we sought in the saguaro forest, for elf owls live nowhere else in the world. From time to time one darted through the night beside us, carrying home to the hungry young a grasshopper or other insect. Some owls held more than one victim, and the assorted legs stuck out around the bird's bill like stiff whiskers. These and the disproportionately large yellow eyes seemed the only landmarks on the smooth little flying ball of feathers.

William Woodin had been our companion previously on a night field trip in a Panamanian jungle, and it was natural that we should compare the tropics with the desert. In the rain forest the bulk of vegetation had been almost invisibly high overhead, so that around us bare holes climbed at intervals from the naked, slippery mud. In the cactus forest the plants were almost entirely subterranean; our feet skidded in the coarse soil, and only the glaring stars told us that the saguaro trunks supported no canopy of leaves. Both regions had their pit-vipers, and lest we step on one, we kept our flashlamps burning. The tropics held fer-de-lance and bushmaster, the desert its own rattlesnakes and those specialists of sandy slopes, the sidewinders.

A few other venom-bearing animals were exploring the night around us. Each used its poison in a different way. Largest and most unique was the two-foot lizard known as a Gila monster. This stout-bodied creature crawled sluggishly over the ground, dragging its short, heavy tail and flicking its black tongue in advance, testing air and soil for prey. Its skin was coarsely blotched with black and pink, and pebbled in a pattern suggestive of the monster's only living relative, the long-tailed Mexican beaded lizard.

Near by, assorted scorpions pranced along. Each held its abdomen high and curved, the stinger ready for defense or offense. Hand-like nippers, similar to those of many crabs, reached forward and explored every crevice for living food.

Trotting about on better than two dozen legs were centipedes as much as eight inches in length. Great tarantulas stalked the desert floor. But the poison in their ice-tong fangs was weak. Their dark furry legs and hairy bodies

199

made them appear far more fearsome than they actually are.

Each of the animals would make way for us if we gave it a chance. Like South Carolina, they wore the simple motto "Do not tread upon me." And their fabled malevolence, as Krutch has pointed out, is primarily defensive: "When a wild animal is described as vicious, it usually means only that if you try to kill him he will sometimes defend himself." Viewed in this light, even a cactus or a rose is dangerous.

Through May the saguaros flower. In June their fruit split open, revealing a red jacket and pulp, set with hundreds of black seeds. They tumble to the ground and there are set upon by rodents, coyotes, birds, and men. The pulp is vaguely sweet. The seeds have thin skins and concentrated nourishment. It is doubtful whether one seed in ten thousand has a chance to germinate.

Other desert plants are correspondingly profligate: the yuccas, shaking seeds noisily from split brown pods; creosote bushes broadcasting their furry white fruit balls; cottonwoods along the dry washes liberating myriads of fluffy seeds into the wind.

Throughout the darkness the long-tailed, leaping mice known as kangaroo rats search out the dry plant products and carry them to underground stores along with bits of stem. Trip after trip fills their huge cheek pouches, and exposes them simultaneously to their many enemies. The kangaroo rat is uniquely American, and one of those creatures able to save the hydrogen and oxygen from carbohydrates and fats, and combine them into the water required for life in dry places. This magic is depended upon by coyote and kit fox, bobcat and badger, spotted skunk and swift-striking snakes which prowl in search of the jumping rodents. For these predators the kangaroo rat is both meat and drink in a parched world.

By moonlight a single separated segment of a cholla cactus suggests a giant tarantula. Where chollas are numerous, pieces are everywhere, for they break off spontaneously or in the slightest breeze. Each is capable of starting a new plant. "Jumping chollas" gain their reputation from the way the segments detach themselves and cling to a mule deer or other large animal careless enough to brush lightly against the parent plant. The weight of the freed branch usually drives its spines into the victim, jabbing the animal into a short run of pained surprise, but one which carries the living cholla segment a dozen yards or more before it is scratched free—to drop to the ground and have its chance to gain a roothold.

Pack rats, which nibble on prickly pear pads, collect cholla segments into great piles. Under these they can scurry from a predator and let the cactus provide a respectable defense. Horned owl, kit fox, and bobcat alike stop at the barrier. A badger may push resolutely into the cholla pile, frightening the pack rat into racing away from the opposite side—often into the waiting jaws of a coyote who has been watching the slow badger's progress.

Just as a saguaro cactus with a deserted woodpecker hole

is a requirement for an elf owl, so also a particular night-flying moth is essential for a yucca plant. The female of the moth *Pronuba* is a specialist at gathering yucca pollen, rolling it into a ball often twice the size of her head, and carrying it from one plant to another. In a second yucca flower, she stabs a few of her eggs into the base of the blossom's ovary and then, with her mouthparts, smears the pollen ball over the surface of the receptive stigmatic tube. The pollen fertilizes all the plant's eggs in this flower, insuring a full crop of seeds. Soon the moth's eggs too begin to develop, and the hatching caterpillars feed on some of the growing seeds. Several weeks later, the caterpillars bore out of the seed pod, let themselves down to the ground on threads of silk, and burrow into the soil. There they pupate and transform into another generation of yucca moths the following spring.

Yucca flowers are just as highly specialized as the moth. The whole stalkful of blossoms forms a creamy white banner against the skies of April and May. But each flower opens in late afternoon, remains accessible to moths through the night, and closes permanently in midmorning. If a few bees get in before dark or after dawn, they contribute little to the yucca's future. The pollen is too sticky to come off easily on a bee's hair, and far too heavy to be disseminated by the wind. The instinctively deliberate actions of the *Pronuba* moth alone fit the adaptations of the plant and insure annual crops of yucca seeds.

Each stalk of desert yucca blooms but once. Those yuccas which bear flowers year after year are the branched "Joshua trees" of the Mojave and nearby deserts. Joshua trees grow thirty to forty feet high, each branch clad in a dense cluster of stiff, sabre-sharp leaves. The plant branches as a means of continuing growth, for whenever a flower cluster is developed to open in the night air, it terminates the stem's advance in that direction. Non-branching yuccas die when their seeds are ripe.

The rate of growth of a yucca flower stalk is so fast as to be almost visible. A foot per day is common, far outdistancing the familiar but smaller asparagus which it resembles.

A similar flower stalk is produced by century plants (aloes of the genus *Agave*) as their final fling in life. They raise the stalk fifteen to twenty feet in less than three weeks. For years each *Agave* has stored water and sun energy in the heavy bases of its long, bayonet-shaped leaves. One leaf may weigh well over two pounds, its green pulp reinforced by stiff white flat fibers similar to those taken from commercial sisal for use in ropes and nets. Yet when the mature leaves reach full development, the aloe squanders all its resources on a gamble for the future. Swiftly it flowers and tempts pollinating birds and insects with nectar and perfume.

Much sugar-rich sap flows into the upthrusting flower stalk, giving energy for the rapid growth. Men have learned to rob the plant. They amputate the bud, scoop out a cavity holding half a gallon or more, and collect the juice as the sweet base for the beer-like *pulque* and the distilled liquor *tequila*. The raw liquid is so attractive to wild animals that the collecting cavity must be covered each evening with the saw-edged leaves, or coyotes will drink it dry.

Other plant denizens of the desert wait for night before unfurling their buds. The various kinds of night-blooming cereus clamber over other vegetation or lie prostrate on the dry soil. Mexican peasants believe that these plants time their flowering to match San Juan's Day—June 24, the supposed birthdate of John the Baptist. Actually they open a few blossoms each night for a protracted period in late spring. Each flower begins to spread its water-lily-like petals about sundown, and in an hour or so is fully open. Around the many yellow-tipped stamens the glistening white petals may spread as widely as fifteen inches across. The blossom liberates a powerful fragrance into the darkness. Hawkmoths whirr to this perfume across the desert, feast on the freely proferred sugar water, and accomplish pollination for the plant. The Indians name this cactus the "Desert Queen," and mention it in many of their legends.

The desert is full of audible calls. Most varied are the excited falsetto yippings of alert coyotes, seated or standing with muzzles raised toward the dark sky. Sometimes two of these wild dogs of desert and prairie will voice a duet, singing so many parts, filling the night with such contrapuntal yelps that a listener suspects the presence of a whole choir. The choristers may be half a mile off, but in the open country and clear air, distance vanishes and they seem only yards away.

Apparently many animals are misled by sounds in arid lands. Heat and dry air together must modify the way sound travels there. Evidence of special needs in hearing may be found in those longest-eared of desert animals, the black-tailed hares—known popularly as jack rabbits. Not only are these the fastest runners of the rabbit kind (to 45 miles per hour) and possessed of a tail so extended (to four inches) that it can leave a track of its own, but their black-tipped ears are remarkably long. They are longer, in fact, on animals from very dry regions than on those living in more humid surroundings, such as along the Gulf Coast of Texas. Five and a half inches is a good average ear length for dead animals of the Mohave Desert, and field studies imply that the ears are even longer while alive.

This superlative ear development is not a feature of the newborn desert hare. A jack's ears do not begin really to extend until an age of some ten days. Prior to this time, except for the conspicuous tail, the young hare could be mistaken for a fully grown Arizona cottontail—the less common desert

representative of true rabbit kind. Yet here too the ear length is greater wherever humidity is low. Cottontails frequent the dry washes, the cat's claw thickets, the scrubby vegetation at the base of canyon walls. There they spend the day hidden in branching burrows, and conceal their young which, rabbitlike, are born blind and almost hairless, unable to leave the nest for several weeks.

Just behind the ear opening on a mammal's head is a thin-walled, bony bulge protecting internal portions of the ear. These bubble-like prominences are much larger in desert hares than in races of the same animal living where the air contains more water vapor. Since hares and rabbits depend upon their hearing rather than upon sight or smell, their ear development must be a reliable guide to the ease or difficulty of detecting direction and distance from a suspicious sound.

Of particular importance to rabbits and hares are noises which might indicate movements of their special enemies, the coyotes and bobcats. Both of these step along silently while searching food. Occasionally a bobcat lifts its voice, alerting the native community with calls just a larger version of those a house cat makes. But otherwise the coyote and bobcat themselves are listening, seeking in the night air a guiding sound to show where hunting might be profitable. Nor do they disdain such small food as mice, lizards, and insects.

Little chirps may be detected as a three-inch gecko scampers across the soil from one cactus clump to another. These small lizards hold their tails up and forward, as though imitating scorpions. The harmless appendage is expendible. If some enemy seizes it, the tail is dropped, to squirm and distract while the lizard itself escapes. The original tail of a gecko is spotted like the creature's body, but replacement tails are plain. However, it is the animal's vocal cords that make it unique among desert lizards. The gecko alone possesses the wherewithal to sing in darkness.

One of the desert mice has earned the name of "calling mouse" for its habit of voicing in the night. This is the grasshopper mouse, a small-bodied, short-tailed, big-eared hunter of insects, scorpions, and even geckos. At intervals, particularly during mating season, these mice raise their heads, close their eyes, open their mouths, and give a prolonged shrill whistle.

Desert is dry but not deserted. While cars race by night over highways crossing the parched land, more animals are active than at any daylight hour. By stopping almost anywhere and walking out into the wasteland beyond the sound of traffic, you may meet creatures adapted for life where liquid water is almost a curiosity. It would be hard to imagine a homeland farther removed from the ancestral seas in which the earliest living things began. Yet the voices of the desert night show how well the dry lands have been colonized by lesser animals.

FOURTEEN

Along the Sea Beach

EARTH has few sanctuaries so meaningful to the human mind as a lonely shore, facing the sea at night. As William Beebe pointed out, it is the "wildest place left in the world, the truest no-man's-land," for no one can stay in the intertidal zone through any twenty-four-hour period unless "anchored and in a diver's suit."

By night the world's daytime dimensions vanish in the sea's white rim of foam. The Milky Way becomes a high bridge spanning the ocean. Below it at intervals may pass the riding lights of coastal steamers. Yet a finger dipped in the ocean is in endless communication with the Atlantic and the Pacific, with the frozen Antarctic and Arctic, the warm Caribbean and Mediterranean, and by way of rivers, with most of the inland lakes as well.

Perhaps it is the contrasts which make night at the ocean's edge so full of stimuli. When fog rolls in and the shore line

shortens to a yard or two in each direction, darkness becomes almost as perfect as in a cave. An ocean transforms into a disembodied sound, like a giant heart pulsing slowly. At the offbeat a tubful of suds flows from nowhere over the sand, only to sink in or drain away. Except for the great bull horn at a lighthouse, moaning a long sad call each minute, it would be easy to conclude that the universe had disappeared.

Closer inspection of the water's edge reveals companions. Fragments of seaweed wash back and forth, evidence of the beds of greenery anchored to the bottom beyond the surf. As each wave pushes up the beach with a sprinkling of sand, half-inch coquina clams may kick themselves energetically from the bottom by the hundreds. The receding water rolls them down the slope, then leaves them in a trailing film of moisture. In this they suddenly upend themselves and vanish downward again by skilful manipulation of the tongue-like foot. With the next wave the sequence repeats itself.

Somewhere in the margin of a little pond left behind by the tide, a stream of water may rise up, curve in a graceful arc, and flow steadily into the pool like a full-scale imitation of a drinking fountain. It comes from a six-inch crab which has buried its body and legs in the sand until all is flush with the surface. Busily it soaks in water from its surroundings, extracts the oxygen, and spurts the residue into the air.

From time to time a two-syllabled clear whistle tells of night activity along the shore. That timid relative of the killdeer, the piping plover, is feeding at the water's edge. Even by day this bird remains so inconspicuous, and its calls come from such deserted beaches, that the name "mourning bird" is commonly given it. But its presence, like that of the crab, the coquina clams, and the seaweed gardens, should be reassuring. As William Morton Wheeler said: "Why animals and plants are as they are, we shall never know; . . . but that apart from the members of our own species, they are our only companions in an infinite and unsympathetic waste of electrons, planets, nebulae and suns, is a perennial joy and consolation."

Most denizens of tidal beach and of shore line beyond reach of ordinary wave action are small and camouflaged. As individuals they are seldom noticed. At night, however, such large populations may be active as to amaze a visitor examining the water's edge with a flashlight. Only a rookery of nesting sea birds or a wave of fiddler crabs on a tropical beach give the same impression by day as the abundance of nocturnal creatures feeding side by side.

The profusion of beach fleas is especially astonishing. In the artificial light, tens of thousands of these flattened crustaceans leap excitedly. All sizes are present, from babies an eighth of an inch long to oldsters nearly a full inch in length. Those on the wet sand are dark brown *Orchestia,* which hover around low-tide mark and feed on microscopic organic matter left by the receding water. Hopping over the dry sand higher up the beach are whitish *Talorchestia.* Both creatures walk slowly as they search for food, but in any commotion they use their last three pairs of legs and tail as a spring which can toss them into the air to a height many times their own length. At a heavy human footfall, all of these creatures begin bouncing from the sand like popcorn in a hot pan. By day they burrow into the beach, often leaving above them a multitude of downward-directed holes pocking the exposed surface as though someone had marked the sand with small sticks ranging in size from toothpicks to pencils.

Each kind of animal inhabits a narrow belt along the shore. Wingless brown earwigs *Anisolabis* range between the line of drift debris to the water, hiding from any light under fragments of wood or seaweed, then prowling at night over the sand. Ten feet beyond the intertidal zone, on shore washed only during storms, the smaller tan earwig *Forficula* grows wings and sometimes uses them to fly to street lamps or lighthouses. *Forficula* hunts for insects among the coastal grass clumps and seems to be a sociable creature. By contrast, the larger seaside earwig *Anisolabis* is a cannibal. Both of these strange insects use the pincers which tip their shining abdomens for fighting and courting, and for defense when needed. Many a picnicker has been nipped by an earwig in the dark when donning a jacket or sweater against the night's coolness. Earwigs explore any object left on the sand, and collect under a garment or in its sleeves and pockets, seemingly grateful for the heat it retains.

From high-tide mark into the sand dunes which mount between the beach and consecutive vegetation, thousands of holes may be open in the early evening, ranging from the size of a pencil to a tunnel large enough to engulf silver dollars. Steeply they slant downward into the sand. Each is the

front hallway of a U- or J-shaped burrow dug by that "rabbit of the crustaceans," the ghost crab. From Long Island to Rio de Janeiro, these creatures emerge at dusk. Each pushes before it the daytime plug of sand which concealed its home and kept intruders from the door. Eight bowed legs, hair-fringed and strong, support the egg-shaped body and its two pincers, one large and one small. A pair of cylindrical compound eyes stand attentively erect, unless the crab chooses to lower them quickly into protecting grooves along the body edge and wipe them clear of sand with a finger-shaped extension from the mouth parts.

Young ghost crabs, which would have to stretch to straddle out beyond a dime, live nearer to the water than do "giants" with bodies three inches wide and a reach exceeding eight. Oldsters have hibernated several winters well below frost line in the deep sand of the dunes. Youngsters have landed only recently after early stages spent swimming in the sea. But

214

every night when the weather is warm enough for activity at all, each ghost crab walks on its eight legs down to the water's edge and waits until a large wave washes in. The final foam of the stalled wave wets the crab's body, seeping under its shell and moistening the walls of an empty chamber where gills are found in most crustaceans. This ritual insures the crab against desiccation for another day or two, and keeps in good condition the surface through which it exchanges carbon dioxide for oxygen. Few crustaceans of comparable size are so thoroughly adapted to life in air.

The wetted crab scampers back to drier land. Between its mouthparts the current of air fanned forward for respiration blows bubbles which burst with faint snapping sounds. Soon all of the ghosts collect along the water's edge and use the smaller nipper as fork and spoon to find, seize, and transfer to the complex mouth a great assortment of tidbits gleaned from the wet sand. The speed and dexterity with which the armored pincer is used vouch for its sensitivity and muscular control. Touch alone guides this feeding in the dark.

By day, ghost crabs are so wary and fleet that the first scientist to describe one from America caught his specimen by running it down on horseback! By night they are easy to approach and show no fear either of the unfamiliar flash-lamp or of gentle footfalls. Probably their severest enemies are gulls which pounce upon any ghost active after dawn, and fish which seize them if they venture too far into the water while wetting their breathing chambers.

In late spring, male ghosts do stately battle on the beach—

feinting and snatching with the larger pincer, or folding it against its base to fret a dozen pegs on the palm of the big claw against a ridge, producing a rasping stridulation. At any time of year, males can be recognized because the folded abdomen, curled tight against the body underneath, is narrow as a G-string. Females, by contrast, wear a broad apron, and throughout the spring, carry in it the fertilized eggs until they hatch. Each night these mothers risk their lives in the shallow water to lower the apronful of young and rinse them off. Wastes from the eggs are washed away, and the developing embryos have an opportunity to soak up needed moisture. Finally each bursts from its thin shell and swims away, leaving the mother temporarily burdened only with a mass of empty eggs glued to her apron lining.

Toward dawn the ghost returns to its burrow and engages in improving the apartment. Every crab must be its own earth-mover. At the entrance it hesitates an instant only— just time enough to fold the eyes into their protective grooves. The ghost goes sidling into the depths with the small pincer leading the way. Soon the crustacean is back at the doorstep, and pauses there to raise the eyes for a preliminary glance around, drop them down for a thorough wiping, and elevate them once more. If the coast is clear, the crab advances another step or two. Only the four leading legs (on the side with the big pincer) provide traction. The opposite group are fully occupied by a handful of sand hauled from the depths. If nothing moves to frighten the watchful animal, it suddenly contracts the cupped legs and throws the sand several times the body length away from the burrow. Before dawn even this mound of fill may be leveled so completely that, when the hole is plugged, no sign remains to show the door's location except a radiating maze of tracks left by the sharp feet.

Alarmed ghosts race for home and vanish down the tunnel. In this rapid running the hindmost pair of legs is raised well off the ground, so that only six participate. The trail they leave upon the beach is noticeably different from that produced when all eight walking legs move in sequence on a scouting expedition. If startled too far from the tunnel mouth to reach it in one excited dash, a ghost will drop into the first burrow large enough—and debate its right to stay a while if the owner is at home. Or the sprinting crab may stop suddenly on soft sand and work all ten of its appendages horizontally, sinking the body below the surface, leaving only the two upright eyes to watch its pursuer hurry by. This ability to disappear one way or another is so characteristic that the name of ghost is well applied. Even by day, the sand-colored body held over the sand is less conspicuous than the shadow it casts with the help of a morning sun.

Neither horse nor flashlight is required for catching ghosts. We have dug dozens from their hideaways using a big clam shell. So entertaining are these crustaceans that we often bring them home as house pets. William Beebe found the same delight: "knowing a crab intimately. . . . We soon come to overlook the structure of crabs, their outer facies, stalked eyes, numerous legs, their sidewise gait, the unyielding

217

external skeleton, and in species and even individuals we perceive personality and a ridiculously manlike outlook on life."

Although crabs as house pets do introduce sand into domestic arrangements, their entertainment value is almost inexhaustible. Unless a large, wire-roofed terrarium is available, they invariably get free and demonstrate unbelievable agility in climbing draperies to hide in valence boards, exploring the recesses of radiators to drag out fuzzy wads of dust, vanishing over the tops of volumes into a bookcase. But they learn from experience to make progressively better shallow burrows in a sand-filled dish. Each night they wait more willingly for a medicine dropper filled with sea water to be brought to their mouthparts and wet their breathing chambers. Ghosts become adept at taking moths from human fingers. Often we have brought them the insects which flew to the screen door. Only fireflies were rejected—apparently bad tasting.

In no other way could we have watched so comfortably the table habits of a ghost—holding a miller in one pincer while tearing off its wings with the other. Using either claw with exquisite control, the crab conveys small fragments of meat to the mouth. Or, stretching the food between the two nippers, it brings powerful jaws to bear on tough membranes and connective tissues. A beetle soon becomes only a heap of shell fragments.

Scavenging the dark beach along with ghost crabs are more timid crustaceans, the hermit crabs. Each carries a snail shell on its back, maintaining in this way a firm covering for the long soft abdomen and a portable cave into which to retreat from danger. Norman Berrill has described these beach-combers as "all front and no fortitude, with all the pugnacity and nervousness of a coward, weapons and armor in front and only vulnerable tenderness behind."

So important is the shell that hermits miss no opportunity to inspect a new one. With claws and feelers they explore thoroughly the recesses of each empty shell encountered. If it seems large enough and uninhabited, the crab slips quickly from its own limy case and pushes its body into the sub-stitute—trying it for fit. The shell seems no burden, since hermits frisk about on the sand in jerky runs. Their borrowed armor makes them relatively immune to wave action, and when the tide comes in, many of them wander off into deeper water for the day.

On the beach at night, a stranded fish or a cracked coconut

is sure to attract an appreciative group of hermit crabs. A small hole through a coconut husk, so long as it gives access to the meat within, can tempt a dozen of these crustaceans. Often their rattling inside is audible many yards away. If their feast is disturbed, they may fairly boil out of the opening, to scamper off or to tumble to the sand and play dead— well drawn back into the shell.

On a northern beach, the crab population is part of summer life. In the tropics, the continuous warm weather permits the crustaceans to be active in every season. But to many a shore in the torrid zone, one special week is almost given over to crabs. Then the land crabs pour by the thousands from rocky hills well inland, and disturb the sleep of all who are active by day. Each crab traveling shoreward is a female, carrying a load of developing eggs about ready to hatch. Clattering and rattling against one another, the mother crabs race through the night toward the sea. Often they clamber over obstructions which could easily be detoured, as though they were following a compass bearing and to deviate a degree would be to get lost. The hordes rush over the beach and into the water. There each crab lowers her apron and the minute, shrimp-shaped young burst from the eggs within seconds. The adults return to their homes almost as rapidly as they came. Months later, when the babies released into the waves have reached crab form and larger size, these too migrate into the hills. But since they are small and their quiet travels are spread over a month of nights, few people notice them.

Land crabs must reach the ocean to liberate their young. Other animals need land on which to lay their eggs. Between the two habits, a beach sometimes becomes a meeting place— a site of considerably congested traffic.

Some of the nocturnal visitors of sea beaches are ponderously large. Each year sea turtles such as the loggerhead and green approach the shore. The big females pull themselves over the sand at night, and select a site well beyond wave action yet within view of the surf. There they dig with their paddle-like hind legs, preparing a deep cylindrical pit into which they can drop fifty to two hundred eggs. One egg dents another, for the leathery shells deform with ease. Finally the mother buries them all by pushing sand into the hole. When the beach is level, she heads back to sea, leaving often a perfectly straight trail from the hiding place to the water's edge.

After about seven weeks the young turtles hatch. Within the nest cavity they mill around for several days. Sand falls from the roof and gradually is added to the floor of their chamber, as though they were on a slow elevator rising toward beach level. The final emergence of young turtles usually occurs at night, yet they find their way to the water through the use of their eyes. Moonlight helps them greatly. But even without it, they detect the white fringe of foam along the surf and run rapidly toward it. They may need to travel twenty-five yards to reach the water. Ordinarily they make no mistakes. Even if the sea is dead calm and no moonlight is available to help them, every one not caught by crabs will strike out for the ocean in the early dawn. Once in, they swim away from shore—if hungry fish do not seize them immediately. This travel from nest to open sea is perilous. If it is tried by day, shore birds get almost every tardy straggler, finding baby turtles an acceptable substitute for fish.

Fish too make use of the sandy shores as a place for eggs. Those who have visited Greenland or other arctic coasts

washed by the North Atlantic know from experience how great are the schools of nine-inch, smelt-like caplins which rush the beaches in spring. Offshore they wait in the night for the highest tide. Then, in a concerted frenzy, they swim with each wave right onto the shore. In a flash they discharge and fertilize their eggs on the beach and turn with the same wave to be carried back to sea. Sand displaced by the water covers the eggs enough to give them some protection. But so many fish participate in this mass reproductive effort that the beach becomes a "quivering" mixture of eggs and sand.

Many animals feast on caplin eggs. Yet millions of the eggs

are able to mature in the sun-warmed sand and are ready two weeks later, when the high tide again washes their area of beach. Into the waves they pop, and swim off to the cold seas.

Southern California's coasts know a close relative of the caplin—the grunion. Because of its more accessible location, thousands of people find an opportunity to watch, wonder, and profit from its similar behavior. On the second, third, and fourth nights after a full moon in March, April, May, and June, cars may be parked bumper to bumper along the coastal highway from the Monterey Peninsula southward. These are the nights when schools of grunion—mostly one-year-olds—approach the beach to lay. When high tide has reached its peak, these six- or seven-inch fish swim into shallow water and let the waves throw them on shore in little groups. A female wriggles her tail to sink into the wet sand until only the front third of her body is exposed. There she lays her eggs. One to three males accompany her. Over her body they arch themselves, and deposit sperm suspension to fertilize the eggs. All this effort occupies only the half minute or less between one wave and the next. With the succeeding breaker they return to the sea.

Since the tide is receding and for the next two weeks will not return inland so far, only a storm would be likely to wash out the eggs. Actually, some sand is deposited over the eggs by the lower tides of succeeding nights, so that they come to lie four inches rather than two below the surface. Sand-probing birds such as the godwit are less likely to find them. Temperature changes, desiccation, and abrasion become less dangerous.

In the dark of the moon two weeks later, tides come in still farther. Waves pound down on the beach where grunion eggs lie buried. These embryos will not emerge without the agitation of the water. For several days they have been ready enough. Now they practically explode from their shells, wriggle up through the soaked sand, and ride the waves into the open ocean.

Grunion and caplin can be successful only along coasts where the highest tides occur at night. Their style of spawning would be too dangerous by day. In the dark a stranded fish is fairly safe from the interval between two breakers. On the few recorded occasions when something has gone wrong with the grunions' clock, so that they have spawned at high tide by day, gulls and other shore birds have gorged on them until each could scarcely fly. Then the birds stood around and merely stared at the fish they could not swallow.

One aspect of caplin, grunion, and sea-turtle activity seems clear: each places the eggs where rain can reach them. A significantly larger percentage of these eggs hatch and develop when the salinity surrounding them is less than that of sea water. Turtles obviously are land reptiles which have invaded the sea. Caplins and grunions, like smelt and salmon, belong to a group of fish all of which migrate at spawning time into fresher water. Even the salmon-like trout of ponds and lakes enter feeder streams to lay. Possibly all fish which move at mating time into shallower water, whether they enter

river mouths (as do smelt and shad) or merely approach the coast (as do herring and mackerel), demonstrate an ancient attachment to fresh water. Perhaps, in the distant past, their ancestors were stream and lake fish. They may be relatively recent additions to the sea rather than ocean fish which are slowly establishing themselves in fresh water.

The fossil record is not complete enough to explain the origins of definite types of fish. But science has fitted together the history of another kind of animal—the horseshoe crab—which uses sea beaches as spawning grounds. Properly this is not even a crab, but is related more closely to scorpions and spiders. Since Devonian times—"The Age of Fishes" some four hundred million years ago—its body form and probably its habits have remained almost unchanged. During those millennia, fishes have been modified enormously. The horseshoe crab is unchanged—a "living fossil."

In spring, full-grown horseshoe crabs move into shallower water. At night their bodies may bulge from the sea's surface like so many brown inverted wash basins as they push themselves over the intertidal flats. There they search for seaweed and worms, young clams and other small soft food. The "cow" crabs are the elders of the population; some of them measure sixteen inches across. The more active males seldom exceed half this width. In both sexes the armored body is hinged transversely behind the middle, and the second part carries a long pointed tail spine. The upper surface of the dome-shaped animal is fairly smooth. Two large compound eyes bulge from the forward portion, and a pair of simple eyes mark the middle of the "forehead."

Even the mode of eating is unique, for the horseshoe crab *Limulus* chews with its spiny shoulders. It has no jaws whatever. Six pairs of jointed legs arise around the mouth, centrally below the forward segment of the body. When water buoys the animal, it walks along the bottom with a curious bobbing gait. The first five pairs of legs lift it from the surface while the hindmost pair provides intermittent shoves. The lifting legs end in points, but the shoving pair are equipped with a ring of coarse flattened spines which prevent them from being driven far into the mud. They are the ski poles with which *Limulus* pushes itself along.

When the bottom is soft or the tide exposes a horseshoe crab to the night air, the animal's body sinks into the surface and the poling legs thrust it forward like a living bulldozer. Having the shell's rim well into the mud must help in deflecting waves which might overturn a crab. In shallows this protection is important, since an inverted crab is almost helpless without the buoyant aid of water. Dawn may come before the ocean liberates it from its awkward position. Then gulls arrive and tear the animal apart, attacking from the one surface where they can get a hold on something soft.

In deeper water, *Limulus* often transforms its bobbing walk along the bottom into free swimming, with legs and gill plates flapping in sequence. The tail spine helps thrust the crab from the bottom and into a sharp U-turn until the creature is cruising along, back downward. Fair distances may be covered in this inverted swimming before movement ceases and the argonaut settles quietly to the bottom again. The shape of the shell causes the body to alight in the same upturned position. But promptly the tail presses against the sand and flops the animal over onto its feet.

Although a horseshoe crab's eyes are sensitive enough to be useful in illumination no brighter than moonlight, it seems evident that the cow crabs attract their mates not by their appearance but by means of a flavorful chemical substance liberated into the dark coastal water of a spring night. The males rush to each mature female. The little "bulls" have hook-shaped knobs tipping the first pair of legs below. With these they grapple for the final flaring taper of the female's shell, just in front of her tail. Once fitted in place, the male is pulled passively wherever his mate goes—ready at any time to pour fertilizing milt over the eggs she lays. A second male may find her lure so irresistible that, if he cannot displace the first mate from his anchored hold upon her shell, he is willing to take second place in the procession. The cow tows them both along—and sometimes three or four—like the tail bows on a kite.

As the night's high tide reaches its peak, ready *Limulus* cows drag themselves and mates onto the shore, and work their bodies well into the sand. Only the first or second male may show above the surface as she pours out her ten thousand greenish-blue translucent eggs, each about two millimeters in diameter. Eels may push their pointed snouts into the mud to gobble up the eggs. The crabs pay no attention. By comparison with the antiquity of horseshoe crabs, both eels and gulls are newcomers. Perhaps they will vanish before *Limulus* does, as did the trilobites, the sea scorpions, and the swimming dinosaurs.

Newborn horseshoe crabs lack the tail spine and resemble extinct trilobites. They burrow shallowly in the mudflats, molt to adult form, and continue to grow while feeding on microscopic plants and animals sifted from the oozy bottom. Mortality due to gulls is high during these early stages, since the body is neither dark colored enough to be inconspicuous (except on clean sand) nor thick enough of shell to resist a bird's strong beak. Those that survive molt time after time, increasing rapidly in dimensions and in armor plating.

Not all of the sea creatures which come up on the beach do so from choice. The overspilling waves may rain thousands of little fish upon the shore—a living surf of herring or of sand eels. Behind them in the breakers, hundreds of small sharks rush back and forth, snapping at the frightened school. Sometimes the pursuers are cod or haddock. On other occasions a herd of seals or of sea lions may produce the same panic. A wave may catch the predator as well, and throw it up on the shore. A dogfish or a "perfectly good" cod will lie there, dying exposed to air. Crabs and gulls clean up the smaller victims. The larger ones remain intact, carcasses left by the receding tide.

A transient record of night activities is spread along the beach in the light of early dawn. Here, a sea turtle plodded away from her hidden eggs. Behind her stretched a broad flat trail, edged with symmetrically repeated patterns like those of bold wallpaper borders. There, a piping plover skittered over the dark sand, leaving a string of crowfoot markings well spaced in almost straight lines. Between each spread print and the next, a streak shows where the middle toe dragged briefly, as though the bird did not step high enough. Farther down the beach, a mouse galloped out of the dunes, down to the driftwood scattered along the shore. Its footprints remain as oval depressions, one oblique pair after another.

Glistening in the low sun, a narrow flat trail was left by a snake. Perhaps it was seeking mice as it wound regularly in a smooth line, progressing inch by inch. The spoor of snake and mouse cross at many points. No doubt the reptile tested the night air repeatedly, flicking out a forked tongue to draw a "sniff" into the sensitive recesses of the mouth.

Occasionally, white-tailed deer emerge from the woods behind the dunes, and walk down to the ocean's edge. Skunk and muskrat are frequent beachcombers. A skunk leaves a neat, almost cat-like trail, where each foot was set down deliberately, its claws slightly spread.

Crabs weave all the other trails together, as they explore the darkness. Short parallel lines mark each ghost's path, the bowed form of each leg accounting for the distinctive streak at each step. Hermit crabs frequently rest in a position so that their shell house touches the sand and leaves a broad mark. The beach fleas, or sand hoppers, are too light to make more than a slight dent when they jump. Shallow pock marks in the sand between the storm wrack and the farthest advance of high tide are often visible traces of their activity. By day their holes are far more conspicuous.

To learn from their spoor the kinds of animals using the sea's rim at night, the naturalist should walk along at dawn. The sun will dry the dew. A light breeze generally springs up. Tracks recording nocturnal enterprises vanish before gulls and bathers begin to stalk about, and sandpipers join early sanderlings in feeding along the ocean's edge.

FIFTEEN

The Coming of Dawn

WITHIN reach of modern man is the means to see clearly outdoors at night, without adding light of any kind. The energy is already available. Rattlesnakes use it to find their prey in the dark. Beyond the reddest red visible to man are wavelengths that we detect as heat if the intensity is high. This energy emanates from most objects around us in the night. If a very sensitive instrument were built—comparable in use to the facial pits of rattlesnakes but designed like a television camera—we could study the midnight world with ease.

Through such an instrument, mammals and birds would shine brightly, because of their high and constant body temperature. Frogs and salamanders would seem densely black—absorbing heat in evaporating water from their moist skins. Ponds and streams would be even blacker. The soil and rocks and plants would all stand out, contrasting with each other according to the rates at which they yielded toward the dark sky the sun's warmth, accumulated through the day. As night progressed, this glow would dim progressively. Seen by its thermal radiation, night would in fact be darkest just before dawn.

With the special camera, it would be easy to understand why a poet might wrongly conclude that "soft falls the dew." Actually dew neither falls nor rises. Water vapor from the night air condenses a molecule at a time on any object whose temperature falls low enough. The drop in temperature is limited if loss of radiant heat is restricted. A roof or even a leaf is enough to reflect the radiations back toward earth. These coverings, if they are exposed toward the sky and space, can become chilled and dew-spangled as though they intercepted moisture falling from above. Below them all may be dry, but only because they served as a shield for heat loss—for heat we cannot see or feel or measure directly.

The air itself may become laden with water droplets. Each droplet carries an electrical charge and repels its neighbors since they are similarly charged. Unless a wind springs up and dashes the charged motes together—mechanically forcing them to fuse—they may hang over the earth as a fog and never turn to rain. The low cloud will also reflect radiant energy back toward the earth, and may prevent formation of dew below it. Even though the air feels humid, the vegetation can remain dry.

When another day stands on the brink of creation, fog may

hide the east completely, but it cannot conceal the imminence
of change from dark to dawn.

If dew has formed, the first faint light sparkles from drops
weighting the work of spiders which have been busy all
through the night, engineering their insect-traps. Some snares
are organized loosely, as a maze of strands to which most

people correctly give the name "cobwebs." Others are woven
into complicated platforms, funnels, doilies, domes. Or they
consist of great vertical nets, the orb-webs, with the radiating lines serving as guy ropes to trees and bushes. A single
spiral strand of sticky silk laces the net together. On it the
spheres of clear water hang in row upon row until gravity
drags them down or a drier air reabsorbs them later.

Dew rarely forms on the bodies of live animals for they
are too much warmer than their surroundings. But glossy

leaves, grass blades, and many animal products are smooth and shiny. They radiate away their heat so rapidly that they grow cooler than the night air, and chill it into giving up its water.

Moisture may be added to the track of a snail. Everywhere the animal's flat foot creeps along, following the lead of the waving tentacles, a mucus film remains as a "serpentine sheen," which Thomas Hardy likened to the streak from a varnish brush marked lightly across the foliage.

Once we watched one of these small, night-active mollusks glide to the tip of a leaf and reach out into space as though seeking another foothold. Farther and farther the shell-less snail extended beyond the end of the leaf, until most of the animal's two-inch length hung head downward. Even then the creature did not halt. Instead it conjured from a gland at the rearmost tip of its foot a heavier ribbon of mucus, and let itself down at the same slow pace. At last it reached a leaf some inches below the starting point. Without hesitation the animal swept slowly away and vanished among the foliage. Behind it the vertical rope remained, gradually becoming beaded with dew.

Like dew, spider silk is typically a product of darkness. It arises from liquid pools within glands carried at the rear of each spider. The glands differ in the shape of the tubes leading to the outside, in the diameter of the thread produced, and in the uses to which their silk is put. Some furnish strands upon which a spider lets itself down, much as the slug did. Others are used in web construction. Still others furnish the delicate threads in which a spider hides her eggs. Seven different kinds of these glands are known. No spider possesses fewer than three, and most have four varieties.

The diameters of the different fibers range from a thousandth to a ten-thousandth of an inch—a third to a thirtieth the size of a human hair. Yet the coarser size of spider silk will support a tenth of an ounce without breaking. This represents a tensile strength of 60,000 pounds per square inch—comparable to the best steel wire if it were drawn out to corresponding fineness.

Spider silk far outshines the similar product of the silkworm. It is uniform throughout, not coated over with sericine as is the caterpillar's thread. The silk scarcely oxidizes, and is resistant to changes in temperature and humidity. These advantages are important to the spinner when condensation loads a web with heavy drops of water.

In the minutes before dawn, another use for spider silk often appears. If just the right amount of breeze springs up, little spiders may climb to some eminence and face the wind. Then they whip up a tangled mesh of silken strands and float it out behind—a sheet of gossamer. Eventually this parachute drags so strongly on the moving air that the spinner is pulled from its perch, to go sailing off across the countryside. Gossamer showers and the spiderlings they carry have been discovered high on mountains and far at sea, spreading the parachutists widely before the sun comes up.

Spider webs and glossy objects are not the only things that develop liquid spheres in darkness. In marshy places on a humid night, jewelweed shows the source of its name when beads of water form from notches along the edge of each leaf. The liquid is not dew but a plant secretion that glistens jewel-like when it is touched by light.

Water secreted by plants such as jewelweed and condensed from the air on cool objects raises the night's relative humidity toward the saturation point before dawn. Just as no two successive midnights ordinarily reach the same temperature, so the relative humidity on one night is seldom repeated exactly on the following. Nor is the slow increase in humidity regular enough or sufficiently rapid to be detected reliably by any animal. Yet during the darkness preceding morning twilight, many creatures behave as though they knew how long it would be before sunup—as though they had an alarm clock running accurately on standard time.

Thus the approach of dawn can be recognized by a practiced eye from the color of a live fiddler crab's body—even if the crab has been maintained for a month or two in total darkness. These creatures are pale at night, dark by day, and continue their rhythmic changes in time with the sun. Once set, the clock runs indefinitely. It even includes a separate timing system, shown by extra blackness, which marks when the tide is low—every twenty-four hours and fifty minutes. When crabs from different beaches are caged together in a laboratory, each maintains its local custom which shows in its coloration when low tide reaches its native home.

Internal rhythms afford an explanation far better than the traditional one for the rising of early birds. Restlessness and song are evident long before morning twilight has reached their roosting places. The timing is the same on an overcast morning as when the sky is clear. Automatically, it seems, the owl's hoot, the muskrat's splash, the rustle of a raccoon foraging, all vanish with the passing of the night.

For animals of land and shallow water, the busiest hours are those at sunset and sunup. These are the times for the changing of the guard. Creatures active by day, depending on vision to find their food, take the place of those at large through the night. During the minutes of twilight, almost every individual is alert and active. In the confusion of transition, the quick-eyed predators snatch many meals.

As the clover leaves unfold and the growing light reflects in each dewdrop, the bat hurries to find its cranny, the owl its tree-hole, the nighthawk its rooftop. While dandelions open, the moths settle on bark, or like fireflies, cling inconspicuously below a leaf. Butterflies and bees and flies will take their places. Worms draw back into the soil and beetles retire below stones and rotting logs.

Crayfish sidle into crevices—from which their name is supposedly derived. Eels and lampreys anchor themselves to some shadowed stone. Along the beach the gulls arrive, the beach fleas dig in, the ghost crabs vanish down their burrows, and the earwigs hide among the drift debris. In the open waters, the small crustaceans dive or sink passively through the brightening water, and the sardine-sized herrings disperse for the day.

In the desert the sidewinders hasten below the surface, the elf owl disappears into a big saguaro, and the pack rat curls up among its trophies under a heap of cholla segments.

Tropical denizens trade places too: larger herds of white-lips where small bands of collared peccaries pawed through the dark hours. Army ants unroll their columns and the birds follow to catch any grasshopper trying to escape by flight. In the arctic, where night yields to day at a pace requiring months for completion, the ptarmigan and the varying hare grow brown in patches; the migrant birds return.

As the dim light of dawn spreads across the sky, a robin hesitantly begins a lonely solo. Speckle-chested thrushes start up: the veery near settled communities, the olive-backed in the woodlands, the gray-cheeked singing its way toward the polar lands. Bluebirds lisp and warble.

An early butterfly may flit across a clearing through the

twilight. Or to columbine and lobelia may come a humming-bird, bent on draining blossoms of any nectar accumulated during darkness.

High above, a woodcock may rise into the brightening sky to carol a love song that blends with the musical whirring of his wings. Warblers join the chorus, adding little excited chirps and snatches of song, searching the brighter side of tree trunks and leaf surfaces for bugs and sleepy flies. Nearer habitations, chimney swifts perform in aerial circus, wheeling aloft and diving, matching the rapid beat of long wings with a staccato twittering.

Most of the birds are wide awake but have not yet left their perches. Night still lingers among the undergrowth in which their food is hiding. But as the sun appears, these notes die away like a conversation when dinner is served. The birds are far too busy eating, breaking the night-long fast and gathering food for their young.

By the time the deer have settled in the thickets, the water birds have drifted quietly away from shore. The hare is in its form, the rabbit in its burrow, the raccoon and opossum and porcupine in their favorite trees. The beaver is asleep in its thatched castle. The mud turtle floats at the pond surface, and frogs are ready for any insect that creeps or flies their way.

In the rhythm imposed by the spinning earth, the world of darkness has yielded. Its stars are lost in the brightening sky. The moon pales. The life-giving sun has overtaken perennial night, to which each cycle returns.

REFERENCES

Page
1   Titus Lucretius, *On the Nature of Things,* trans. by Cyril Bailey (Oxford: Clarendon Press, 1910), book V, 11.956–85.
2   William Shakespeare, *A Midsummer Night's Dream,* Act IV, Scene 1.
6   Archibald Rutledge, *Children of the Swamp and Wood* (New York: Doubleday, Page & Co., 1927), p. 52.
8   W. H. Hudson, *Far Away and Long Ago* (New York: E. P. Dutton & Co., 1926), p. 206.
13 D'Arcy W. Thompson, *On Growth and Form* (2nd ed.; New York: The Macmillan Co., 1948), p. 53.
21 Rudyard Kipling, "Mandalay," from *Barrack Room Ballads and Departmental Ditties* (Calcutta: Thacker & Spink, 1888), end of refrain.
22 Henry Wadsworth Longfellow, "The Day Is Done," from *Longfellow's Poetical Works* (London: Geo. Routledge & Sons, Ltd.), p. 273, stanza 1.
35 Lincoln Barnett, "The Woods of Home," from *The World We Live In, Life,* November 8, 1954, p. 78.
37 Henry D. Thoreau, *Walden,* ed. by Edwin Way Teale (New York: Dodd, Mead and Co., 1946), p. 193.
47 E. Lawrence Palmer, *Fieldbook of Natural History* (New York: McGraw-Hill Book Co., 1949), p. 619.
50 William Shakespeare, *Macbeth,* Act II, Scene 1.
51 Mary Webb, *Poems and The Spring of Joy* (New York: E. P. Dutton & Co., 1929), p. 154.
54 Robert Louis Stevenson, *Travels With a Donkey* (London: 1879), p. 219.
55 W. H. Hudson, *Birds in Town and Village* (New York: E. P. Dutton & Co., 1920), p. 144.
67 Henry David Thoreau, *op. cit.,* p. 185.
69 Mary Webb, *op. cit.,* p. 117.
70 Hal Borland, *An American Year* (New York: Simon & Schuster, 1946), p. 46.
87 Henry David Thoreau, *op. cit.,* p. 137.
88 Aldo Leopold, *Sand County Almanac* (New York: Oxford University Press, 1949), p. 18.
89 William Beebe, *Unseen Life of New York* (New York: Duell, Sloan & Pearce, 1953), p. 9.
95 J. Henri Fabre, "The Life of the Caterpillar," from *The Insect World of J. Henri Fabre,* ed. by Edwin Way Teale (New York: Dodd, Mead and Co., 1949), p. 81.
96 Bence Jones, *Life and Letters of Faraday* (2nd ed.; New York: Longmans, Green & Co., 1870), Vol. 1, p. 116.
107 Aldo Leopold, *op. cit.,* p. 18.
107 Frederick C. Lincoln, *The Migration of American Birds* (New York: Doubleday, Doran & Co., 1939), p. 77.
109 Ludlow Griscom, *Modern Bird Study* (Cambridge: Harvard University Press, 1945), p. 66.
111 William J. Beecher, *Scientific Monthly,* July, 1952, pp. 23–24.
113 Frederick C. Lincoln, *op. cit.,* p. 23.
117 Gilbert White, *A Natural History of Selborne* (London: B. White & Sons, 1789), pp. 125–26.

REFERENCES

Page

119   Robert J. Newman, *Studying Nocturnal Bird Migration by Means of the Moon* (University, La.: Museum of Zoology, Louisiana State University, 1952), p. 11.

119   Alfred Noyes, "The Highwayman," *Blackwood's Magazine,* Vol. 180 (August 1906), p. 244, first stanza.

119   William Beebe, *The Log of the Sun* (Garden City, N.Y.: Garden City Publishing Co., 1906), pp. 94–96.

128   *Holy Bible,* King James Version, Exodus 16: 11–13.

131   Charles Darwin, *The Voyage of H.M.S. Beagle* (London: J. M. Dent & Sons, Ltd., 1930), p. 155.

135   Alexander Agassiz, "The Islands and Coral Reefs of Fiji," *Bulletin of the Museum of Comparative Zoology,* Harvard University, Vol. 33, pp. 16 *et seq.*

166   William Beebe, *High Jungle* (New York: Duell, Sloan & Pearce, 1949), p. 214.

166   Archie Carr, *High Jungles and Low* (Gainesville, Fla.: University of Florida Press, 1953), p. 6.

167   H. W. Bates, *The Naturalist on the River Amazons,* (5th ed.; London: John Murray, 1884), p. 32.

167   H. M. Tomlinson, *The Sea and the Jungle* (New York: The Modern Library, 1928), p. 183.

168   Robert Louis Stevenson, "The Beach of Falesá," from *Island Nights' Entertainments* (New York: Charles Scribner's Sons, 1895), p. 309.

173   William Beebe, *High Jungle* (New York: Duell, Sloane & Pearce, 1949), p. 174.

176   Paul Russell Cutright, *Great Naturalists Explore South America* (New York: The Macmillan Co., 1940), p. 298.

177–78   Frank M. Chapman, *Life in an Air Castle* (New York: Appleton-Century Co., 1938), p. 179.

178   Paul Russell Cutright, *op. cit.,* pp. 107, 110.

182   William Beebe, *Jungle Peace* (New York: Henry Holt and Co.), p. 154.

182   Louis J. Halle, Jr., *River of Ruins* (New York: Henry Holt and Co., 1941), p. 76.

183   Henry W. Bates, *op. cit.,* pp. 32, 140.

183   Paul Russell Cutright, *op. cit.,* p. 143.

187   Theodora C. Stanwell-Fletcher, *Driftwood Valley* (Boston: Little, Brown and Co., 1946), p. 134.

194   Aldo Leopold, *op. cit.,* p. 23.

200   Joseph Wood Krutch, *The Desert Year* (New York: William Sloane Associates, 1952), p. 214.

209   William Beebe, *Jungle Days* (New York: G. P. Putnam's Sons, 1925), p. 52.

212   William Morton Wheeler, *Science,* Vol. 57, January 19, 1923, p. 71.

217–18   William Beebe, *Nonsuch, Land of Water* (New York: Blue Ribbon Books, 1932, pp. 185–86.

219   N. J. Berrill, *The Living Tide* (New York: Dodd, Mead and Co., 1951), p. 160.

232   E. L. Beers, "The Picket Guard," *Harper's Magazine,* September 30, 1861, stanza 6.

234   Thomas Hardy, *Far from the Madding Crowd* (New York: Harper & Brothers, 1918), p. 285.

INDEX